INVERNESS

Highland Town to Millennium City

INVERNESS

Highland Town to Millennium City

Norman S. Newton

breedon **books**
PUBLISHING

First published in Great Britain in 2003 by
The Breedon Books Publishing Company Limited
Breedon House, 3 The Parker Centre,
Derby, DE21 4SZ.

ISBN 1 85983 356 X

Printed and bound by Butler & Tanner,
Frome, Somerset, England.

Cover printing by Lawrence-Allen Colour Printers,
Weston-super-Mare, Somerset, England.

CONTENTS

ACKNOWLEDGEMENTS

I would like to acknowledge the assistance and co-operation of the staff of the Am Baile project (www.ambaile.org.uk), a consortium of partners in the Highlands and Islands of Scotland led by The Highland Council, particularly in providing photographs from the Highland Photographic Archive, which is curated and administered by Lesley Junor. Thanks also to the staff of Highland Archives and Highland Libraries, especially in the Reference Room at Inverness Library. Thanks to the many students who enrolled in WEA and KEY Learning Opportunities (Aberdeen University) courses over the years, and who opened my eyes to the enthusiasm which local history studies can generate. I am grateful to Stuart Brownlee, former Head of Libraries and Archives with The Highland Council, who encouraged me to embark on this project, and to current colleagues in Highland Libraries, who encouraged me to complete it. Thanks also to the editorial staff at Breedon Books, who patiently coped with missed deadlines and adopted sufficient flexibility in the production process to accommodate them. Finally, thanks to family and friends, and apologies to Lizzie, for ignoring her for so long.

INTRODUCTION

THIS book is an introduction to the history of the City of Inverness, focusing particularly on the last 200 years. However, the earlier history is not entirely neglected and the first two chapters of the book consist of a summary of the previous 5,000 years of human occupation.

It was during the Middle Ages, in the years between 1100 and 1600, that Inverness became a town and an important centre of trade and commerce. The strategic position of the town was the determining factor in its growth, but without formal authorisation from central government in the form of official Charters from the Kings and Queens of Scotland, the Burgh of Inverness could not have flourished in the way that it did. Even so, it was not until the last quarter of the 19th century, with the arrival of the railway, that it became clear that Inverness rather than, for example, Cromarty, Dingwall or Elgin, was going to become the main trading port and administrative centre in the north of Scotland.

The first rail link was to Nairn, connecting through to Aberdeen and the south, in 1855. In 1863 the Highland Railway reached Inverness, providing a direct route to Aviemore, Perth, Glasgow, Edinburgh and London. It took a while for Invernessians to realise the full implications. Inverness was now a railway town, but without much of the required infrastructure. Tourist hotels, guide books, tour operators, specialist shops and services – all had to be developed. Inverness had accommodated tourists since the 18th century, including Daniel Defoe, James Boswell and Samuel Johnson and a succession of aristocrats from France and Germany, but never in the numbers now about to descend on the town. Apart from the spin-off of tourism, the Highland Railway in itself became one of the major industries in Inverness. Hundreds of men – and women – worked for the railway and dozens of local families who were involved as Directors or shareholders followed its fortunes closely. They were not disappointed and for some it made their fortunes.

Hard on the heels of the Highland Railway came the redevelopment of the town centre, with single-minded Victorian entrepreneurs sweeping away what remained of mediaeval Inverness. Ironically, some of the grander Victorian buildings would, in their turn, be swept away by town planners in the 1960s – leaving the opportunity for imaginative redevelopment in Bridge Street as one of the challenges for the new City of Inverness in the 21st century.

In 1831 official statistics gave the population of Inverness as just under 10,000 and throughout the first half of the 19th century it increased steadily, reaching 12,500 by 1861. Then, in the 30 years up to 1891 the population of the Royal Burgh of Inverness grew by almost a further 10,000, in the boom years caused by the coming of the railway. By 1901 the population of the burgh was 21,000. By 1961, as local government and administrative agencies grew, it had crept up gradually to 30,000. Then, in the 30 years up to 1991 there was another rapid population growth, to nearly 42,000, or to over 50,000 if the new housing estates around Smithton, Culloden and Balloch are included. The recent 2001 Census showed a further increase, to 55,000 – still small for a city but Inverness continues to be one of the fastest-growing areas in Britain.

The City of Inverness is now the administrative centre for the Highlands, with the headquarters of many organisations. It is the engine driving economic growth for the whole of the Highlands and a cultural, educational, artistic and literary hub for the Highlands.

Recent years have seen an explosion of interest in local history in the Highlands and nowhere has this been more productive than in Inverness. The Inverness Field Club, founded in 1875 , regularly attracts audiences of over 100 to its lectures and operates a programme of historical excursions during the summer months. Reflecting an astonishing growth of fascination in our personal ancestries, the Highland Family History Society also attracts large audiences to its monthly meetings and runs genealogical workshops in Inverness Library. Most of its members, once they have exhausted the obsessive nature of family history, develop an interest in the historical and social conditions in which their ancestors lived and worked. The work of the Highland Family History Society, particularly its transcriptions of Highland gravestones, provides the skeletal framework which for many people is the beginning of an understanding of Highland history. Its website reflects its worldwide membership

On perhaps a slightly more 'cultural' level, the Gaelic Society of Inverness focuses on the culture of the Gaels and again attracts healthy audiences, both to its monthly lectures and to its website. The Society was founded in 1871 to foster the Gaelic language and the history, literature, music and traditions of the Highlands. Although it aims to encompass the entire Highlands and Islands, the Transactions of the Gaelic Society of Inverness include many papers relating, in one way or another, to the history of Inverness.

More recently, the Inverness Local History Forum, a branch of the Scottish Local History Forum, was formed and, through its 'Inverness Remembered' programme, is endeavouring to record the memories of aged Invernessians on tape, for posterity. With the support and encouragement of Inverness Museum, these tapes are transcribed and preserved, old photographs collected and exhibitions mounted. Its monthly meetings are also well attended, often attracting audiences of over 100.

Supporting and underpinning these societies are the facilities of Highland

Libraries and Highland Archives, currently based in the former Farraline Park school, adjoining Inverness bus station. Inverness Library has perhaps the finest collection of books relating to the Highland and Islands of Scotland outside of the National Library of Scotland in Edinburgh, much of it due to the generosity of Charles Fraser Mackintosh, MP, whose library of over 5000 books was gifted to the town of Inverness after his death in 1901. The collection also includes the books which formed the core of the Burgh Library of Inverness from the 17th century onwards, sometimes (erroneously) referred to as the 'Kirk Session Library' – because at one time the church authorities assumed responsibility for its upkeep.

As well as this superb collection of books, Inverness Library maintains a collection of Inverness and Highland newspapers on microfilm, with appropriate facilities for making copies. The *Inverness Journal* (1808-1845), the *Inverness Advertiser* (1845-1885) and the *Scottish Highlander* (1885-1898), as well as the still thriving *Inverness Courier* (founded 1817) and *Highland News* (founded 1882) provide the raw material of local history. Detailed card indexes cover the 19th century, with plans in hand to make them available in digital format. This is the kind of material often ignored by academic historians, more interested in national trends, but repays closer examination for the minutiae of local life. Personal triumphs and tragedies abound in the pages of local newspapers, often detailed in scurrilously intrusive reporting which would not be out of place in the modern tabloid press. In an age when the local newspaper was one of only a few forms of public entertainment, Inverness editors took full advantage of their position to keep their readers enthralled – bearing in mind that their readership was not the mass market of today, but the educated section of the population who could read and afford the price of a weekly news sheet.

Sharing the old Farraline Park building with Inverness Library are the understaffed and under-resourced facilities of Highland Archives. They have a statutory responsibility to collect all the records of the Highland Council – and of all its predecessors: Inverness County Council, the Town Council of Inverness, Highland Regional Council and all its constituent District Councils, including Inverness District Council. Highland Archives also collect records and manuscripts in private hands and are always happy to acquire still more material, though current facilities for storage and for research are wholly inadequate. One of the great hopes for Invernessians interested in their local history is that an integrated Local Studies/Highland Archives/Family History Centre with proper storage for the preservation of records and archives, adequate research and study facilities and with an appropriate collection of local books, periodicals and newspapers, will be built in Inverness for the benefit of locals and the many hundreds of visitors from overseas who visit us each year.

Most overseas visitors are, of course, initially interested in their family history. Highland Archives employs one full-time Genealogist, with a part-time assistant, though there is clearly enough potential to keep a much larger team fully occupied. Quite apart from the financial possibilities, there is a cultural responsibility for the Highland Council, with the support of local groups, to provide adequate facilities which allow access to the cultural riches entrusted to its care. Public demand, coupled with a belated realisation by public authorities of their responsibility to the Highland community, make it likely that Inverness will become the proud recipient of a new research centre in time for its celebration of the Highland Year of Culture in 2007.

Also supporting local history in Inverness are the Workers' Educational Association and KEY Learning Opportunities, formerly the extra-mural department or Department of Adult and Continuing Education of the University of Aberdeen. The WEA runs introductory local history classes in Inverness, covering the individual districts and communities of the town and attracts good numbers, many of whom go on to more detailed study. They also run Local History Days in Inverness and surrounding communities, to drum up support and interest in local history. The University of Aberdeen runs a lecture series in Inverness each year, often on local history topics and, for those students who want to explore the subject in greater depth, there is a programme of courses in history, archaeology and cultural studies which can lead to appropriate Certificates and eventually to a university degree. It is anticipated that the University of the Highlands and Islands will become increasingly involved in local history, through its constituent colleges and institutions.

For ordinary people, it has never been easier to do local history. Libraries, archives and museums are now totally committed to widening access to their holdings. Television and radio programmes promote an interest in history and archaeology, while increasing access to the internet means that family history can now be unravelled from the comfort of a living room, where in previous generations it was the unique preserve of the aristocracy. This democratisation of local history, through the commitment of public institutions and through the wonders of the world wide web, has created an irresistible demand.

In the Highlands, the Am Baile/Gaelic Village project, which aims to make material relating to the history and culture of the Highlands freely available over a website, gives us a glimpse of how local history might be done, worldwide, in the 21st century. Of particular interest to the general public are the many thousands of images available through this digital medium: etchings, engravings, book illustrations and early photographs from the Highland Photographic Archive, many of which are published for the first time in this book.

Environment and Early History

THE 'Millennium City' of Inverness was created by Royal Warrant in the year 2000. The Royal Burgh of Inverness dates from the early Middle Ages, but as a strategic settlement at a geographical crossroads in the north of Scotland, there has been a centre of population at the head of the Moray Firth since prehistoric times.

Inverness lies at the northern end of the Great Glen, a rift valley, geologically ancient and relatively inactive. From time to time earth tremors are felt in Inverness and very occasionally stronger earthquakes shake the town. The earthquake felt all over Scotland on 13 August 1816 damaged the steeple of the Tolbooth, twisting it out of alignment. It was not repaired until 1828, by which time it had become an object of curiosity, comparable to the Leaning Tower of Pisa. The Tolbooth survives to this day on Bridge Street – all that remains of the original Court House and adjoining prison.

Because the Great Glen is steep-sided and flat-bottomed, and runs from coast to coast, it has been a natural route for human communication since the end of the last Ice Age, when the land was re-colonised, some 10,000 years ago. The first farmers, the Neolithic people with their stone axe and flint technologies, arrived around 3500 BC and began to tame and settle the landscape. They built massive communal burial places, chambered tombs, of which the cemetery of three cairns at Clava, just outside Inverness, is a ritual landscape of cairns and standing stones which was in use for many centuries, perhaps up to the end of the Bronze Age in the Highlands, around 1200 BC.

Just to the north-east of Raigmore Hospital, near what, in ten years time we are told, will be regarded as the centre of Inverness, there are the remains of a circular cairn of the Clava type, fairly common around this part of the Moray Firth. However, it is not in its original position – when the new A9 road was being aimed like an asphalt arrow at the new Kessock Bridge, the cairn was moved from the path of the advancing highway to save it from obliteration and re-erected in its present location. It narrowly missed a similar fate a century earlier, when the railway line into Inverness passed close by. Only the stone kerb of the cairn

survived, all the stones having been robbed away over the centuries for use in building works and stone dykes in the area.

When it was on its original site the Raigmore cairn was known as the Stoneyfield (or Achnaclach) stone circle. But even its new name is not exactly as it seems. Raigmore Hospital is one of the defining institutions of Inverness and we take its name for granted – but the farm lands on which it is built were originally named Broomtown, not Raigmore. It takes its name from the estate purchased in the 1820s by Lachlan Mackintosh of Raigmore, who renamed his lands after the hovel up country, near Tomatin, where the neighbouring settlement of Raigbeg is still signposted. Unravelling landscape history is never straightforward but always revealing.

If the Raigmore/Broomtown/Stoneyfield/Achnaclach cairn is therefore decidedly dodgy, though reasonably sympathetically recreated, it is undeniable that the cairns at Clava are incomparably more impressive. Nobody wishing to get just a little way inside the heads of our Neolithic ancestors can give them a miss. Three cairns survive, none of them completely intact but all with most of their original cairn material still present. All have the diagnostic kerbstones (which is all that remains at Raigmore). Additionally they are surrounded by circles of standing stones, which may or may not be contemporary, some with inscribed decorative patterns. With passages aligned on the Bronze Age midwinter sunset and situated in shady groves, they are amongst the finest monuments of the period anywhere in Scotland. They are in the care of Historic Scotland and well provided with interpretative panels. Regrettably, as has been reported in local newspapers, some of the 'druidic' night-time visitors who flock to the site during the major festivals of the Celtic calendar, often leave bits and pieces of paraphernalia and litter which are cleared up by the authorities. Occasionally building work within Inverness has revealed traces of early settlement, in the form of burial cists (stone-lined graves with capstones) and stray finds of prehistoric objects. In prehistoric times much of what we think of as Inverness would have been boggy land, subject to regular flooding; settlement would have been on the fringes of the flood plain of the River Ness and on the slopes and higher ground to the west and east.

One such settlement was Craig Phadrig, the Iron Age hill-fort whose distinctive profile overlooks Inverness from the west, above the houses of Scorguie. It was excavated in the 1970s, providing evidence of Iron Age occupation inside its spectacular ramparts and ditches. The discovery of a secondary Dark Age occupation confirmed local traditions of a Pictish fortress, perhaps occupied during the time of King Brude, who confronted St Columba when the holy man and his entourage visited Inverness in the 580s – and sighted Nessie in between encounters with the local 'heathen barbarians'.

However, it has to be said that Craig Phadrig looks very much like an Iron Age fort, dating from the first millennium BC and nothing at all like the typical 'nuclear' Dark Age fortress, with a central defended core on a craggy hilltop, surrounded by a series of defended terraces. There is such a site not far from Inverness where Pictish-age artefacts have been found and which does have the requisite characteristics of a Pictish royal fortress. This is at Castle Urquhart, on Loch Ness, underneath the later medieval castle. Another possible candidate for King Brude's fort is Torvean Hill, overlooking the Caledonian Canal. Unfortunately the fort itself, if indeed it ever existed, was long ago destroyed by quarrying, but the discovery of what has been plausibly been described as a royal grave, with an enormous silver chain, lends credence to this identification.

We know very little of the people who lived in the Iron Age fort on Craig Phadrig, but quite a lot about the folk who occupied the site towards the end of its life – the Picts. First mentioned in classical sources, from about 300 AD the

East cairn, Clava (PSAS, *v. 3*).

Picts were the most important people in this part of Scotland until at least the middle of the 9th century, when, in the words of Isabel Henderson, 'under Viking pressure, Kenneth MacAlpin led the Scots from Argyll into the eastern Pictish districts of Scotland and set up the Scottish administrative centre there.'

Her chapter entitled 'Inverness, a Pictish capital' in the Inverness Field Club centenary volume, *The Hub of the Highlands: the book of Inverness and District* (1975) summarises the evidence for Craig Phadrig as a Pictish administrative centre. The emblem of the Field Club, a Pictish Boar, comes from the Boarstone, a Pictish standing stone located on the southern edge of Inverness, with the outline of a boar etched on the face of the stone.

Inverness Museum has a fine interpretative display on the Picts, with examples of inscribed stones and Pictish artefacts from the area. Groam House Museum, at Rosemarkie on the Black Isle, has a much larger collection of material, including the magnificent Rosemarkie Cross.

Historical research into the Dark Ages over the last 20 years, coupled with archaeological investigations at hill-forts of the period, have given academics sufficient confidence to start describing those times as the 'Early Historic Period'. Perhaps we could concede that the darkness has become a little less gloomy, but it is not likely that such an infelicitous phrase will replace the 'Dark Ages' in the public imagination. The terms refer to that period after the breakup of the Roman Empire, in the early 400s AD, up to the emergence of a Scottish feudal state in the 11th century, as the result of Anglo-Norman invasions in what we have come to refer to as the Early Middle Ages.

Did Columba really visit Inverness and meet King Brude of the Picts? Certainly Columba's biographer – Adamnan, the abbot of Iona – writing perhaps 100 years after Columba's death, believed that he did and wrote a wonderfully descriptive account. In his *Life of Columba* he says that, as Columba was travelling in Pictland, he saw somebody being buried on the banks of the River Ness, a victim of a water monster which inhabited the river. When he ordered one of his followers to swim across the river to fetch a boat from the other side, the monster, 'whose hunger had not been satisfied earlier,' sensed the swimmer's presence:

> 'Feeling the water disturbed by his swimming, it suddenly swam to the surface, and with a mighty roar from its gaping mouth it sped towards the man as he swam in midstream.'

Columba made the sign of the cross and commanded the monster to withdraw:

> "You shall not advance further, nor touch the man. Go back with all speed." Then the beast, hearing these words of the saint, fled back terrified at full speed, as if dragged away by ropes...'

Both the 'heathen barbarians' and the 'brothers' were impressed by this miraculous demonstration of saintly power. Adamnan writes that the locals:

> 'were impelled by the great power of this miracle, which they had seen with their own eyes, to magnify the God of the Christians.'

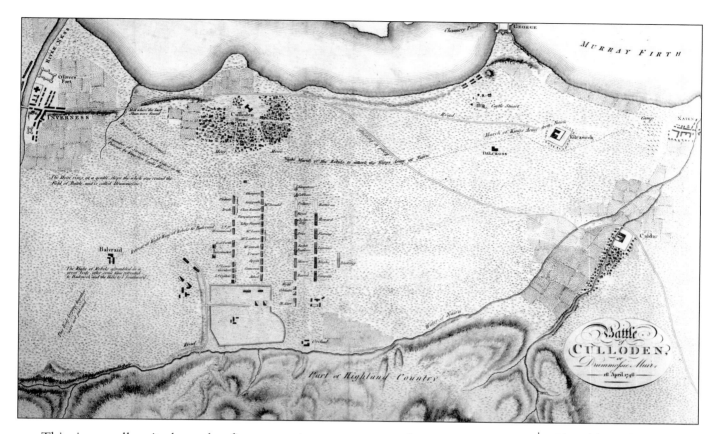

Plan of the Battle of Culloden, from Home's History of the Rebellion.

This is usually cited as the first eye-witness account of Nessie; it has a vividness and immediacy which is impressive. Cynics might point out that river monsters are a well-known feature of the Pictish world, a fact of which Columba (and Adamnan) would have been well aware, so that it would have been in their interest to 'stage' an event where Columba counteracted the power of heathen belief with a suitable miracle. It is also worth noting that this episode took place not in Loch Ness, where Nessie now resides, but in the River Ness. The debate goes on. Sometimes in history what we believe to be the case becomes more significant than what really was the case – perhaps we will never really know where St Columba and King Brude encountered each other, or what really happened when the saintly hero bested Nessie.

Across the Beauly Firth from Inverness, looming above the far side of the Kessock Bridge, is another hill-fort, on the Ord Hill. Typically of an Iron Age fort of the early first millennium BC, it consists of a single rampart and ditch encircling a large summit area on the ridge making up the Ord Hill. Together with Craig Phadrig, this fort guards the northern approaches to the Great Glen and the maritime approaches to Inverness and the Beauly Firth – more proof that the strategic importance of Inverness was recognised in prehistoric times.

At both Craig Phadrig and Ord Hill traces of 'vitrified' material were found in the Iron Age ramparts. This is wall material which has been heated to a very high temperature and has melted, forming a glassy or vitreous appearance, a bit like enamel. Bubbles in the stone caused by super-heated gases are also a feature of this material. 18th-century antiquarians were content to describe vitrified forts and rule out a geological or volcanic origin; in the 19th century they could not

Pictish chain from Torvean burial (PSAS, v. 10).

resist wandering into the realms of speculation as to the reasons for this effect. At one time it was believed that it was a construction technique, creating incredibly resistant walls at key areas of the hill-forts, but more recent research seems to suggest that because the distribution of vitrified material around the walls of forts all over the Highlands is reasonably random, it probably resulted from accidental firing of the ramparts.

At one time it was believed that two Iron Age tribes coexisted in Highland Scotland, one living in vitrified forts and one preferring unvitrified forts. However, research showed that the difference was geological, not cultural. Vitrified forts occur where the geology makes the process possible – where there is sufficient silica in the rock. The effect also depends on the walls being constructed around a timber framework, allowing drafts to develop, creating the heat necessary for the silica in the rock to melt. Another necessary condition was, of course, sufficient wind to create sufficient draft, but windy days have never been rare in the Highlands.

Inverness Museum, located on Bridge Street beside the late-Victorian Town House, has a fine collection of displays relating to the natural history and environment of the area. The public library in Inverness, located at Farraline Park, has many books in which the geology and landscape of the area can be studied. Much of the research is based on the work of local people, first published in the pages of the Transactions of the Inverness Scientific Society and Field Club which, between 1875 and 1924, published many interesting papers based on its meetings and excursions.

A feature of Inverness local history has been the number of interested antiquarians who took an interest in their cultural and historical environment and devoted many years of research to writing up the fruits of their labours. Few had specific archaeological, historical or architectural training, but were nevertheless quite happy to share their thoughts with a wider public.

The most famous of these antiquarians and certainly the most productive, was Charles Fraser Mackintosh (1828-1901). Born Charles Fraser at Dochnalurg, his mother was a Mackintosh of Borlum and on the death, in 1857, of Aeneas Mackintosh, his maternal uncle, he adopted that surname in order to carry on that branch of the family name which otherwise would have died out. There was, of course, a financial incentive in his uncle's Testamentary Deed of Settlement.

Charles Fraser Mackintosh went to work in a lawyer's office in Inverness at the age of 14 and subsequently went to Edinburgh University to complete his education. He became an assistant to the Sheriff Clerk in Inverness and was admitted to the local bar in 1853. He led a distinguished and, presumably extremely profitable, career in the legal profession, then dabbled in estate management for his Mackintosh clan chief, before being tempted into politics, first on the Town Council and then, in 1874, as Member of Parliament for the Inverness Burghs. At the 1885 election he changed constituencies, reflecting his interest in crofting reform, and was elected as MP for the county of Inverness. He was defeated at the 1892 election after a lifetime of public service. He was the only Gaelic-speaking Member.

He was a dedicated collector of material, but a bad historian. His legal mind preferred to accumulate and categorise charters, letters and documents, with often not a very clear idea as to their context. He also had a distressing tendency to dispose of original clutter after he had transcribed documents, leaving us unable to clarify some possible mistakes and ambiguities in his work.

His contributions were widely recognised, particularly in the *Celtic Review*, which helpfully published a long and informative summary of his life and achievements. His library of over 5,000 books was bequeathed to the town of Inverness and, from 1921, on the death of his wife, formed the core of the local collections. Fraser Mackintosh was a great supporter of the Public Libraries Act and made a personal donation to enable the provision of a public library in Inverness at Castle Wynd, which he opened on 12 June 1883, during a break from his exertions on the Napier Commission into the reform of crofting. There are important collections of Jacobite pamphlets and a very comprehensive collection of material relating to the Ossian controversy. There are very few books relating to the Highlands which were not in his personal library. We will have many occasions to refer to his life and work in greater depth later in the course of this book.

Tomnahurich Bridge, prior to 1937 when the present swing bridge was built. The bridgekeeper's house dates from 1813. In the background is Torvean Hill. ©Highland Photographic Archive

THE ROYAL BURGH OF INVERNESS

IT IS difficult to conflate over 1,000 years of history into one chapter, but it was during what we loosely call the Middle Ages that Inverness established its reputation as one of the most important towns in the north of Scotland. From 1603 the Kingdoms of Scotland and England were united and during the 17th and 18th centuries Invernessians, for most of the time, lived the lives typical of residents of a small provincial town in North Britain – with one important exception: the date of 16 April 1746, the date of the Battle of Culloden, is etched on every Highlander's psyche.

At issue that day was the question of whether a Hanoverian or a 'native' Scot would sit on the throne of Great Britain. Hundreds of years before, in the 11th century, in the time of Macbeth, Duncan and Duncan's son Malcolm Canmore, much the same was at stake. Macbeth (1005-1057) killed Duncan and became King of Scotland, eventually losing out to the usurper Malcolm, who with English support defeated him in 1054 at Dunsinane and, in 1057, crushed his final attempt to regain power and killed Macbeth at Lumphanan.

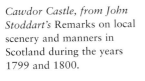

Cawdor Castle, from John Stoddart's Remarks on local scenery and manners in Scotland during the years 1799 and 1800.

During the reign of Malcolm, in 1066, England was invaded by William the Conqueror and it was not long before Malcolm was forced to submit to him, in 1072. Malcolm came to terms with the Anglo-Norman invaders. Later, in the reign of David I, sixth son of Malcolm Canmore's marriage to St Margaret, Anglo-Norman ideas of feudalism and social organisations were espoused fully, in particular the novel idea of trading burghs with Royal Charters.

The history of Inverness in this early period is decidedly murky. The location of 'Macbeth's Castle' in Auldcastle road and 'King Duncan's Well' at Culduthel testify to some likely local connections to these key players in the historical drama of 11th century Scotland, even if those connections cannot readily be traced back prior to the attentions of Victorian antiquarians and have no corroborative documentary or archaeological evidence. It is quite likely that there was a timber Anglo-Norman castle either at 'Castlehill' or underneath the later stone keep overlooking the main river crossing. Perhaps it also needs to be said that Shakespeare's *The Tragedy of Macbeth* is great drama but bad history. Shakespeare was, of course, writing for entertainment rather than historical accuracy and the inclusion of themes of treachery, murder, deception and unbridled ambition certainly ensure captivating drama. Some observers have suggested that there would have been clear resonances for his English audiences as they faced up to the arrival of James VI, of Scotland, on the throne of what, as James I, he insisted on referring to as 'Great Britain'. Most analysts, however, have concluded that the play was written, or adapted, for the amusement of James. Certainly it suggests that Banquo, almost the antithesis of Macbeth in the play and a reputed ancestor of the Stewarts in real life, was one of a long line of kings to come.

The earliest known mediaeval charter which applies to Inverness was issued sometime during the reign of William the Lion, 1165-1214. It grants the right to the Burgesses of the Province of Moray to limit their financial liability to their own personal debts. As most of the burgesses in Moray were in fact in Inverness this is sometimes regarded as the first Burgh Charter.

Because charters were in effect a personal contract between the King and certain of his subjects, they required to be renewed with each successive reign. Thus, we learn that further charters, some now lost, were issued in the reigns of Alexander, David I, James I, James V and Mary, Queen of Scots, the mother of the granter of the so-called 'Great Charter' of 1591, James VI (soon to be James I of Great Britain). This charter confirmed all previous charters and defined the properties and privileges of the burgh. It confirmed the status of Inverness as the most important burgh in northern Scotland and, in particular, made it clear that Inverness had trading and market rights over other northern burghs, such as Dingwall, Cromarty and Tain.

An eyewitness to events in and around Inverness during much of the 16th century was Rev James Fraser (1634-1709), minister of the parish of Wardlaw (now Kirkhill). His account was published by the Scottish History Society in 1905

Cromarty at the end of the 18th century (Stoddart).

as Chronicle of the Frasers, but is often referred to as 'the Wardlaw Manuscript'. His main purpose is to relate the achievements of the Fraser family (his ecclesiastical patrons) but there are vivid accounts of events in Inverness, especially covering the turbulent period of civil war in the 1650s and the 1660s. He was there when 'Cromwell's Fort' was built in 1652 and again ten years later – when it was demolished. The outline of this 'Old Fort' appears in William Roy's *Military Survey of Scotland* (1747-55) and as 'Citadel' on John Home's 1774 map of Inverness. No trace now remains of this Cromwellian fortification – even 'Cromwell's Tower', supposedly the last remnants of the fort surviving as a clock tower, has recently been shown to be a reconstructed fake, probably based on the offices of a local rope factory.

The Welshman Thomas Pennant's account, *A Tour in Scotland*, (1769) contains a short description of Inverness. Approaching from the east, he makes his position clear regarding the events of only 23 years before:

'Passed over Culloden Moor, the place that North Britain owes its present prosperity to, by the victory of April 16th, 1746. On the side of the moor are the great plantations of Culloden House, the seat of Duncan Forbes, a warm and active friend to the house of Hanover, who spent great sums in its service, and by his influence, and by his persuasions, diverted numbers from joining in rebellion; at length he met with a cool return, for his humane but unpolitical attempt to sheathe, after victory, the unsatiated sword. But let a veil be flung over a few excesses consequential of a day productive of so much benefit to the united kingdoms.'

So much for Celtic solidarity!

Pennant continues:

'After descending from the moor, got into a well-cultivated country; and after riding some time under low but pleasant hills, not far from the sea, reach Inverness, finely seated on a plain, between the Firth of the same name and the River Ness: the first, from the narrow strait of Ardersier, instantly widens into a fine bay, and again as suddenly contracts opposite Inverness, at the ferry of Kessock, the pass into Ross-shire.

The town is large and well built, and very populous, being the last of any note in North Britain. On the north is Oliver's Fort, a pentagon; but only the form remains to be traced by the ditches and banks. Near it is a very considerable rope manufacture. On an eminence south of the town is old Fort George, which was taken and blown up by the rebels: it had been no more than a very ancient castle, the place where Boethius says that Duncan was murdered: from thence is a most charming view of the firth, the passage of Kessock, the River Ness, the strange shaped hill of Tommin Heurich, and various groupes of distant mountains.

That singular Tommin is of an oblong form, broad at the base, and sloping on all sides towards the top, so that it looks like a great ship with its keel upwards. Its sides and part of the neighbouring plains are planted, so it is both an agreeable walk and a fine object. It is perfectly detached from any other hill and if it was not for its size, might pass for a work of art. The view from it is such, that no traveller will think his labour lost, after gaining the summit.

At Inverness, and I believe at other towns in Scotland, is an officer, called Dean of the Guild, who, assisted by a council, superintends the markets, regulates the price of provisions, and if any house falls down, and the owner lets it lie in ruins for three years, the dean can absolutely dispose of the ground to the best bidder.'

This passage from Pennant's *Tour* raises many interesting points. He makes

Highland scenery near Inverness, from A history of the Scottish Highlands, Highland Clans and Scottish Regiments, *by John S. Keltie.*

the journey from the Culloden battlefield seem like a long way, which on foot it no doubt is, but today's commuters can be in the centre of Inverness in ten minutes! There is no description of the battlefield itself, though travellers well into the 19th century reported finding musket balls and even swords amongst the heather. Pennant confirms that Cromwell's Fort existed only in outline, five years before it was drawn on John Home's map, which is a prime piece of evidence that our clock tower has more to do with the rope works which Pennant saw than a Civil War fortification. The 'Fort George' he mentions is of course the site of Inverness Castle, overlooking the main bridge over the Ness and not the Hanoverian fortress at Ardersier. Pennant was clearly impressed by Tomnahurich Hill, in his day not yet a cemetery. His advice to the traveller still applies. In a footnote to his original work, Pennant notes that the length of the top of the hill was 300 yards and the width only 20, so one can imagine him pacing it out from one end of the hilltop to the other.

Lieutenant General Wade, Commander-in-Chief of all His Majesty's Forces in Scotland (Keltie).

He has another footnote detailing some of the 'prices of provisions' regulated by the Dean of Guilds:

> 'Beef, (22 ounces to the pound) 2d to 4d.
>
> Mutton, 2d to 3d.
>
> Veal, 3d to 5d.
>
> Pork, 2d to 3d.
>
> Chickens, 3d to 4d a couple.
>
> Fowl, 4d to 6d apiece.
>
> Salmon, of which there are several great fisheries, 1d and 1d halfpenny per pound'

Pennant crossed the Ness 'on a bridge of seven arches' in 1769 and proceeded along the shores of the Beauly Firth and on into the northern part of his Scottish adventure. Returning to Inverness, he was lucky to observe a fair in progress. He had read in Boethius's *History of Scotland* (1527) that Inverness was trading with German merchants, who purchased the furs of wild beasts and that the neighbourhood of Inverness was famed for wild horses; that the surrounding countryside provided a great deal of wheat and other grain; and that 'quantities of nuts and apples' were also traded. Boethius was the Latin name of Hector Boece (1465-1536), the Dundee historian who was appointed Principal of the newly-founded University of Aberdeen. Pennant noted that some things had not changed since the early 16th century:

> 'At present there is a trade in the skins of deer, roes, and other beasts, which the Highlanders bring down to the fairs. There happened to be one at this time... the commodities were skins, various necessaries

brought in by the pedlars, coarse country cloths, butter and meal, the last in goatskin bags, the butter lapped in cawls, or leaves of the broad alga or tang... and great quantities of birch wood and hazel cut into lengths for carts, etc which had been floated down the river from Loch Ness. The fair was a very agreeable circumstance, and afforded a most singular group of Highlanders in all their motly dresses.'

There follows a long and detailed passage which is one of our best sources for local costume at the end of the 18th century. Pennant notes in passing that the gentry wear truish, 'breeches and stockings made of one piece'.

The dress of women, he observes:

'resembles that of women of the same rank in England... but their condition is very different, being little better than slaves to our sex.'

In a now very controversial passage, Pennant passes judgement on what he perceives as the characteristics of the Highland population:

'The manners of the native Highlanders may justly be expressed in these words... indolent to a high degree, unless roused to war, from experience, to lend any disinterested assistance to the distressed traveller, either in directing him on his way, or affording their aid in passing the dangerous torrents of the Highlands... hospitable to the highest degree, and full of generosity... are much affected with the civility of strangers, and have in themselves a natural politeness and address, which often flows from the meanest when least expected. Through my whole tour I never met with a single instance of national reflection! Their forbearance proves them to be superior to the meanness of retaliation. I fear they pity us, but I hope not indiscriminately. Are excessively inquisitive after your business, your name, and other particulars of little consequence to them... most curious are the politics of the world, and when they can procure an old newspaper, will listen to it with all the avidity of Shakespeare's blacksmith. Have much pride, and consequently are Impatient of affronts, and revengeful of injuries. Are decent in their general behaviour, inclined to superstition, yet attentive to the duties of religion, and are capable of giving a most distinct account of the principles of their faith. But in many parts of the Highlands, their character begins to be more faintly marked, they mix more with the world, and become daily less attached to their chiefs... the clans begin to disperse themselves through different parts of the country, finding that their industry and good conduct afford them better protection (since the due execution of the laws) than any their chieftain can afford... and the chieftain tasting the sweets of advanced rents, and the benefits of industry, dismisses from his table the crowds of retainers, the former instruments of his oppression and freakish tyranny.'

Culloden House (Keltie).

In Samuel Johnson's *A Journey to the Western Isles of Scotland*, an account of his travels with James Boswell published in 1785, the famous lexicographer describes arriving in Inverness on Saturday, 28 August 1773 after a fine dinner with the governor of the garrison at Fort Augustus: 'We did not regret the time spent at the fort, though in consequence of our delay we came somewhat late to Inverness, the town which may properly be called the capital of the Highlands. Hither the inhabitants of the inland parts come to be supplied with what they cannot make for themselves hither the young nymphs of the mountains and valleys are sent for education, and as far as my observation has reached, are not sent in vain.'

Johnson recognised that Inverness was at the boundary of what he considered the civilised world, beyond which the trappings of 18th century urban life were indeed in short supply:

'Inverness was the last place which had a regular communication by high roads with the southern counties. All the ways beyond it have, I believe, been made by the soldiers in this century.

We were now to bid farewell to the luxury of travelling, and to enter a country upon which perhaps no wheel has ever rolled. We could indeed have used our post-chaise one day longer, along the military road to Fort Augustus, but we could have hired no horses beyond Inverness, and we were not so sparing of ourselves, as to lead them, merely that we might have one day longer the indulgence of a carriage.

At Inverness therefore we procured three horses for ourselves and a servant, and one more for our baggage, which was no very heavy load.

We found in the course of our journey the convenience of having disencumbered ourselves, by laying aside whatever we could spare, for it is not to be imagined without experience, how in climbing crags, and treading bogs, and winding through narrow and obstructed passages a little bulk will hinder, and a little weight will burthen, or how often a man that has pleased himself at home with his own resolution, will in the hour of darkness and fatigue, be content to leave behind him every thing but himself.'

Like Pennant, whose book he had read, Johnson felt compelled to deliver himself of some observations on the Highland population, while at Inverness:

'I was told at Aberdeen that the people learned from Cromwell's soldiers to make shoes and to plant kail. How they lived without kail, it is not easy to guess: they cultivate hardly any other plant for common tables, and when they had not kail they probably had nothing. The numbers that go barefoot are still sufficient to shew that shoes may be

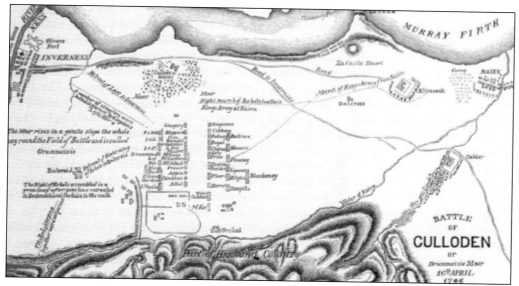

Plan of the Battle of Culloden (Keltie).

spared… they are not yet considered as necessaries of life, for tall boys, not otherwise meanly dressed, run without them in the streets and in the islands. The sons of gentlemen pass several of their first years with naked feet.'

Johnson is impressed with Scottish poetry, literature and the general level of education, but is puzzled by the lack of interest in consumer comforts:

'Yet men thus ingenious and inquisitive were content to live in total ignorance of the trades by which human wants are supplied, and to supply them by the grossest means. Till the Union made them acquainted with English manners, the culture of their lands was unskilful, and their domestick life unformed; their tables were coarse as the feasts of Eskimeaux, and their houses filthy as the cottages of Hottentots. Since they have known that their condition was capable of improvement, their progress in useful knowledge has been rapid and uniform. What remains to be done they will quickly do, and then wonder, like me, why that which was so necessary and so easy was so long delayed. But they must be for ever content to owe to the English that elegance and culture, which, if they had been vigilant and active, perhaps the English might have owed to them.'

Johnson's travelling companion and guide, himself a Scot and indeed the instigator of their great adventure, was James Boswell, whose account of their travels is regarded as a classic of travel literature. It was first published in 1785, after Dr Johnson's death, as *The Journal of a Tour of the Hebrides*. It is interesting to compare their accounts:

'We got safely to Inverness and put up at Mackenzie's inn. Mr Keith, the collector of

Flora MacDonald, the young Scottish girl who won fame for saving the life of Bonnie Prince Charlie after the Battle of Culloden Moor. (Keltie).

Inverness from Pennant's Tour of Scotland, *1769.*

Excise here, my old acquaintance at Ayr, who had seen us at the fort, visited us in the evening, and engaged us to dine with him next day, promising to breakfast with us, and take us to the English chapel, so that we were at once commodiously arranged.

Not finding a letter here that I expected, I felt a momentary impatience to be at home. Transient clouds darkened my imagination, and in those clouds I saw events from which I shrunk, but a sentence or two of the Rambler's conversation gave me firmness, and I considered that I was upon an expedition for which I had wished for years, and the recollection of which would be a treasure to me for life...

Sunday, 29th August

Mr Keith breakfasted with us. Dr Johnson expatiated rather too strongly upon the benefits derived to Scotland from the Union, and the bad state of our people before it. I am entertained with his copious exaggeration upon that subject, but I am uneasy when people are by, who do not know him as well as I do, and may be apt to think him narrow-minded. I therefore diverted the subject.'

Yes, we have all been in that position, especially when discussing the Union! The two travellers visited the Episcopal Church after breakfasting and were not impressed:

'The English chapel, to which we went this morning, was but mean. The altar was a bare fir table, with a coarse stool for kneeling on, covered with a piece of thick sail-cloth doubled, by way of cushion.

Inverness Castle, from Burt's Letters.

18th-century Highland dress (Burt).

Old Town House, built 1708, demolished 1878. ©Highland Photographic Archive

The congregation was small. Mr Tait, the clergyman, read prayers very well, though with much of the Scotch accent.'

After church they walked down to the harbour, then along the river to what they described as 'Macbeth's castle', the ruins of Fort George at the bottom of Bridge Street:

'Just as we came out of it, a raven perched on one of the chimney-tops, and croaked. Then I repeated

"...The raven himself is hoarse,

That croaks the fatal enterance of Duncan

Under my battlements."

We dined at Mr Keith's. Mrs Keith was rather too attentive to Dr Johnson, asking him many questions about his drinking only water.

Having conducted Dr Johnson to our inn, I begged permission to leave him for a little, that I might run about and pay some short visits to several good people of Inverness. He said to me, "You have all the old-fashioned principles, good and bad." I acknowledge I have.

That of attention to relations in the remotest degree, or to worthy persons, in every state whom I have once known, I inherit from my father. It gave me much satisfaction to hear every body at Inverness speak of him with uncommon regard. Mr Keith and Mr Grant, whom we had seen at Mr M'Aulay's, supped with us at the inn. We had roasted kid, which Dr Johnson had never tasted before. He relished it much.'

The only other thing we know about Boswell and Johnson's visit to Inverness in 1773 is that Johnson bought himself a book there. Two days after leaving the town the travellers were at Glenmoriston, where they spent a night:

'We had tea in the afternoon, and our landlord's daughter, a modest civil girl, very neatly drest, made it for us. She told us, she had been a year at Inverness, and learnt reading and writing, sewing, knotting, working lace, and pastry. Dr Johnson made her a present of a book which he had bought at Inverness.'

Cromwell's Tower. ©Highland Photographic Archive

29

Dunbar's Hospital, Church Street (1668), built by Alexander Dunbar of Barmuckety and Westfield, replacing an earlier hospital. There was a grammar school on the ground floor until 1792 when Inverness Royal Academy was built. Later used as parish library, female school and to house fire engines. ©Highland Photographic Archive

The book in question, it turns out, was Cocker's *Arithmetick*, which might seem a strange choice of purchase, but Dr Johnson defended it as Boswell quotes:

' "Why, sir, if you are to have but one book with you upon a journey, let it be a book of science. When you have read through a book of entertainment, you know it, and it can do no more for you; but a book of science is inexhaustible." '

Samuel Johnson's own account of this episode is rather touching:

'We were surprised by the entrance of a young woman, not inelegant either in mien or dress, who asked us whether we would have tea.

We found that she was the daughter of our host, and desired her to make it. Her conversation, like her appearance, was gentle and pleasing. We knew that the girls of the Highlands are all gentlewomen, and treated her with great respect, which she received as customary and due, and was neither elated by it, nor confused, but repaid my civilities without embarrassment, and told me how much I honoured her country by coming to survey it.

She had been at Inverness to gain the common female qualifications, and had, like her father, the English pronunciation. I presented her with

a book, which I happened to have about me, and should not be pleased to think that she forgets me.'

A week later the travellers were on the Isle of Skye, where they were astonished to find vestiges of civilisation and were well looked after. Their account of a couple of days in Inverness and their description of Highland glens and mountains had a significant and long-term effect in persuading other intrepid travellers in the last decades of the 18th century to follow in their romantic footsteps.

Old Town House showing Commercial Hotel to left, where Boswell and Johnson stayed in September 1773. ©Highland Photographic Archive

INVERNESS IN THE EARLY 19TH CENTURY

AT THE beginning of the 19th century Inverness was a small Scottish provincial town, albeit a Royal Burgh. The population was reckoned to be about 5,500 in 1801; by 1821 this had grown to 8,500 and by 1901 to 23,000 – quadrupled in just 100 years. The population of 'Inverness' today is over 50,000 and growing – nearly ten times the size of 200 years ago.

In 1800 Inverness was the effective northern limit for travelling with wheeled vehicles. It was possible to reach Tain, but difficult to obtain houses north of Inverness. There were lots of other tracks, perfectly adequate as cattle tracks or 'drove roads' and for pedestrians or men on horseback, but hopeless for the purposes of commerce. North and west of Inverness trade and commerce depended on sea transport. There were roads down the Great Glen to Fort William, eastwards to Nairn, Elgin and Aberdeen and south through Badenoch to Perth, but there was a crying need for improved communications.

An Act of Parliament for making roads and bridges in the Highlands and for constructing the Caledonian Canal, was passed in 1803. Work began promptly, supervised by the famous engineer of bridges, roads and harbours, Thomas Telford. Explicit in his plans were the aims of improving commerce, promoting fisheries and stemming the flow of emigration.

This period of intense civil engineering projects continued until 1821. In 1807 new bridges were constructed at Beauly, Conon, Contin, Bonar and at The Mound in Sutherland. By 1818 we are told in the Annual Report of the Commissioners who were overseeing Telford's progress on behalf of Parliament, that 'from Edinburgh to Inverness and from Inverness to John O'Groat's House, it is now possible to travel without crossing a ferry or fording a river, or even encountering a descent where the necessity of using a drag chain is required.'

With improvements in the roads came better communication by the mails and better accommodation for travellers. There was an attempt to establish a regular coach to Perth in 1806, but it was 1809 before a successful and reliable service

Inverness, from Thomas Newte's Prospects and Observations on a Tour of England and Scotland *(1791).*

operated, running three times a week in summer and twice a week in winter. In March 1808 there was an advertisement in the *Inverness Journal* for the first carrier north of Dingwall. His name was Donald Ross and he would travel as far as Tain. In June 1809 a 'diligence', as it was called, began to run from Inverness to Tain by way of Beauly and Dingwall. Then, on 5 April 1811, a daily mail coach was established between Aberdeen and Inverness. It was not cheap, however – an inside seat was £3 13s 6d, while outside it was £2 9s.

At this time the mail from London took six days and there is a record of a journey from Edinburgh to Sutherland taking 47½ hours. A mail coach from Inverness to Wick started up in July 1819. It left Inverness at 6am, arriving at Wick at half past seven the following morning – a journey of 26½ hours.

The construction of the Caledonian Canal took nearly 20 years. When the waterway was opened in October 1822 it was found that the total costs had reached £884,000. In the way of these things, the estimated cost had been £474,531. In 1803, day labourers were paid from 1s 6d a day, but by 1814 this had risen to 2s 6d.

Along with the roads and the canal, there were improvements in sea transport for paying passengers in the first 20 years of the 19th century. In 1804 vessels began to ply regularly from Inverness to London, calling at Cromarty, initially once every three weeks and then every ten days. The journey usually took from ten to 14 days. Sometimes it was a lot quicker – In February 1815 the Inverness

Town Steeple. ©*Highland Photographic Archive*

Packet sailed from Gravesend to Burghead in only 70 hours, having outstripped the mail by 34 hours.

In the early years of the 19th century the town of Inverness consisted of little more than the streets now forming the core of the city centre: High Street, Bridge Street, Church Street, Castle Street and New Street (now Academy Street). The Northern Meeting Rooms were built in 1790; the Royal Academy and the Jail and Courthouse in Bridge Street, in 1791. The principal streets were levelled and paved in 1796. In 1798 the Chapel of Ease, later the United Free East Church, was built. In 1803 Thornbush Pier was built and the harbour deepened.

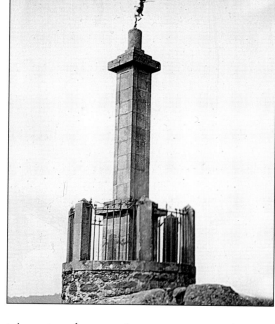

Clachnaharry Monument (1821). ©Highland Photographic Archive

In the year 1800 Dr John Leyden passed through Inverness and formed a less than glowing opinion of the town:

> 'We beheld indeed very little that is not to be seen in every town... it contains some elegant buildings, but no regular streets or squares of neat houses... Many of the houses are of considerable antiquity and have the arms of some Highland chieftain sculptured on a large slab inserted in the wall, from having been the town houses of those chieftains in feudal times.'

Even his description of the view from Craig Phadrig is rather barbed:

> 'The finest view of Inverness is from the eminence above Muirtown as you ascend Craig Phadrick, one of the eminences of that ridge which conceals the Fraser country, or Aird. Here the apparent regularity of the arrangement and elegance of the structures greatly exceeds reality.'

By 1824 Dr Macculloch was a little more appreciative, calling Inverness 'a clean town and a good-looking town ... it possesses the best and the civilest and cheapest inns in Scotland.'

Describing a tour through Scotland in 1798, Dr Thomas Garnett reached Inverness in late July:

> 'Inverness is a large and well-built town, containing some 8000 inhabitants. The houses are very lofty, and many of them elegant. It is very properly called the Capital of the Highlands, there being no other town of any consequence in the north. There are some very good inns: that, where we took up our abode, is kept by a Mrs. Ettles. Our accommodation was very good; we experienced much attention and civility, and were charged very reasonably. Almost opposite to our inn,

Old windmill, South Kessock, built 1827 and used as a flour mill until the 1880s. The remains were removed in 1943. ©Highland Photographic Archive

near the centre of the town, stands the court-house, with which is connected the jail or tolbooth. It is a very handsome modern building, with an elegant tower, terminated by one of the handsomest spires I have seen. The prison is dry, and kept remarkably neat.'

This building replaced an early Tolbooth recorded as early as 1436, while a steeple is first mentioned in 1569.

Dr Garnett also gives us a useful account of the Academy, founded in 1790:

'A piece of ground containing about three acres was purchased, and an elegant building erected, consisting of a large public hall, with six very spacious apartments for the accommodation of the different classes, the Library, and philosophical apparatus. The business is conducted by a Rector and four tutors.'

There was an impressive curriculum: in the first year, English, 'taught gramatically'; in year two, Latin and Greek (in a premonitory misprint, the 1811 edition of Dr Garnett's journal uses the word 'Geek' for perhaps the first time!); the third year covered arithmetic and book-keeping. Building on these basics, year four covered geometry, geography, navigation and practical astronomy; naval, civil and military architecture; practical gunnery; perspective and drawing. In their final year, in the Rector's class, students tackled 'civil and natural history, experimental philosophy and chemistry'. 'Experimental philosophy' is what we would call physics.

The 200-300 students paid fees ranging from 6 shillings in the first year, 12 shillings in years 2-3, a guinea (21s) in year four and a guinea and a half in the final year, as well as an additional annual fee to the Rector. The school year was divided into two terms: from 16 July to 20 December and from 5 January to 10 June.

Two hundred years ago it was already recognised that the Gaelic language needed promotion: the Highland Society of London sponsored a class for teaching the language, paying £15 a year for a tutor, to which the directors of the Academy added a further £16.

Dr Garnett would have been pleased to see, 200 years later, the establishment of the University of the Highlands and Islands (UHI), giving this assessment of the value of the Academy to Inverness and the Highlands:

> 'Though it has not the name, it possesses most of the advantages of an university, and may serve as a place of complete education for all, excepting those intended for the learned professions, who may here lay an excellent foundation, and raise the superstructure at Edinburgh or Glasgow.'

Apart from the Academy there were several other schools and charitable institutions in Inverness in 1800. During Dr Garnett's visit the public subscription which established the Northern Infirmary in 1803 was being actively promoted. As a medical man himself, Dr Garnett took an interest in the health of the Highlands:

> 'I was informed, by an eminent medical gentleman in Inverness, that cancers are very common in this country, particularly among the labouring class of people, which he attributes to their manner of living, and particularly to the use of whisky. This complaint here chiefly affects the lips, tongue and nose and it may be owing to the callosity induced by bringing the unadulterate spirit so often in contact with them, which destroys their irritability. Perhaps snuff and tobacco, which are much used in the Highlands, may contribute their share.'

The chief industries in Inverness in 1800 were hemp and flax. Hemp processing employed over 1000 men, women and children. It was imported from the Baltic and made into sail-cloth and sacking. Flax processing, says Dr Garnett, 'is said to employ, in all its branches, such as heckling, spinning, twisting, bleaching and dyeing, no less than 10,000 individuals in the town and surrounding country.'.

It too was imported, mainly from the Baltic and the resulting white thread sent to London and then exported all over the world.

To support the manufacturing industries there was a healthy shipping industry to carry the goods to the markets in the south, principally to London. In addition they carried locally-caught fish caught and 'the skins of otters, rabbits, hares, foxes, goats, roes, etc'.

The fish caught were mainly herring and sprats.

In 1798 Highland dress was still common:

> '…and is undoubtedly much more picturesque and beautiful than the formal, tight, stiff habit of the English and Europeans in general. The highland bonnet is in particular very ornamental; so are the graceful folds of the plaid. The modern habit has, however, convenience to recommend it, and in a few years this ancient dress of the highlanders, which resembles very much that of the ancient Roman, will probably be scarcely seen.'

Dr Garnett noted that both English and Gaelic were spoken 'promiscuously' in the town of Inverness in 1798, though the language of 'the country people' was Gaelic. As with other writers, he was impressed by the standard of English spoken in the town 'with very great purity, both with respect to pronunciation and grammar'.

He attributed this mainly to the fact that for most people English was not the mother tongue, but learned 'by book'. He also agreed with others that 'the garrisons of English soldiers which have been in the neighbourhood since the time of Cromwell have in a great measure regulated the pronunciation.

At the end of his time in Inverness Dr Garnett visited 'Craig Phatric' and was impressed by its setting and its vitrified ramparts, before leaving the town by way of the battlefield of Culloden, today established as part of the tourist itinerary of the Highlands. Provost John Mackintosh escorted him round the battlefield, showing him the graves where the clansmen had been buried:

> 'In one which had been opened a few days before, we saw several human bones. The country people often find small cannon- and musquet-balls, which they sell to the curious who come to take a view of this field of battle.'

Provost Mackintosh evidently briefed his visitor well:

> 'The behaviour of the soldiers, after the victory at Culloden, will always be a stain both upon the army and their commander; they refused quarter to the wounded, unarmed and defenceless; many were slain who had only been spectators of the combat, and the soldiers were seen to anticipate the executioner.'

In the *Old Statistical Account* of the parish of Inverness, written in 1791, the ministerial authors comment on how, after 1746, the economy of the Highlands gradually started to recover, after a long period of decline. Particularly in the most recent 30 years, they say, there has been 'a rapid progress of improvement.'

*Clachnaharry Monument.
©Highland Photographic
Archive*

The *Old Statistical Account* describes the civic government of Inverness at the end of the 18th century in some detail. There was a Town Council of 21 members, elected every Michaelmas, with a clerk and clerk-depute. From these Members were elected a Provost, four Bailies, a Dean of Guild and a Treasurer. There were six guilds of craftsmen in the town: Hammermen, including smiths, tinsmiths, coppersmiths, silversmiths, watchmakers, braziers, cutlers and saddlers; Wrights, including house-carpenters, cabinet-makers, wheel-wrights and coopers. The others were Weavers, Tailors, Shoemakers and Skinners. Other crafts which were not organised into guilds included masons, cart-wrights, bakers, butchers and barbers.

According to the *Old Statistical Account* there were 52 prisoners in the Tolbooth in 1790:

'Horse-stealing	30
Petty thefts	8
Threatening expressions	4

Alleged willful fire-raising	1
Scandal and defamation	1
Deserting apprenticeships	3
Alleged murder (boy)	1
Violent assaults	3
Child murder	3
Selling spiritous liquors without a licence	1
Women of bad fame	2
(for irregularities and misdemeanours)	
Breach of the peace	5
Deserting His Majesty's Service	1
Civil debts	17
Total	52'

The authors of the *Old Statistical Account* are quite complimentary in their assessment of their parishioners:

'The inhabitants of the town and parish are decent, and regular in their attendance on the public ordinances of religion. They are well affected to the government of their country, good neighbours, and industrious in their several occupations. Instances of dissipation and profligacy are rare.'

Of craftsmen living in the town of inverness, the *Old Statistical Account* says that:

'Their houses are clean and neat, and their boards abundantly provided with animal as well as vegetable food. Tea equipages, in their opinion, are now become necessary.'

The 19th century got off to an explosive start in Inverness in 1801 when a large quantity of gunpowder blew up in the town centre, killing seven people and injuring many others. Many houses were damaged and had their windows shattered. In 1807 a gunpowder magazine, paid for by the Burgh, was built at the Longman.

On 9 October 1807 the *Inverness Journal* records that an emigrant ship bound for Pictou in Canada had cleared customs at Thurso, with 130 men, women and children. Noting that it was hoped that the Caledonian Canal, then under construction, would attract local labour and so reduce or hopefully eliminate the need for emigration, the editor notes that 'none were under the necessity of leaving their native country'.

He adds:

'Most criminal infatuation! That can thus lead men to migrate from their native homes into a state of voluntary banishment, peril, and toil the most laborious, to a country where they have not only to toil, but to make the field, the half of which exertion and labour would have made the country they thus abandon pregnant with every blessing.'

On 25 December, in the same issue which records the purchase of the Cradlehall estate by Charles Grant MP for £7950, a correspondent from Thurso brings news that the brig *Pampler* had been wrecked near the Bay of Bulls in Newfoundland with the loss of 138 lives. Only three passengers survived. There is no comment from the editor. Subsequent reports suggested that most of the emigrants were not from Sutherland, as first noted, but from Caithness.

The Tolbooth spire that so impressed Dr Garnett was damaged in the earthquake which shook Inverness on Tuesday 13 August 1816, at 10.40pm. It is recorded in the *Inverness Journal* of 16 August:

> 'Some of the inhabitants who had retired were suddenly tossed out of
> their beds, and many were horribly alarmed by the universal shaking
> of the houses, the rattling of the slates, and the tremendous crash of
> large stones which were precipitated with violence from many of the
> chimney tops. Happily, however, from the lateness of the hour very few
> persons were then in the streets, and consequently no lives were lost.'

It was reckoned the event lasted 20 seconds. It caused great consternation, with people rushing half-naked into the streets. Next day the damage could be assessed:

> 'In the morning it appeared that the beautiful spire attached to the Jail
> was, at the distance of several feet from the top, completely rent and
> twisted several inches round, in a direction from the east towards the
> north-west.'

The spire was repaired in 1828.

In an amazing piece of serendipity, we have an eyewitness account of the earthquake of 1816, by one of the very few female excursionists to have left a

Original timber 'Black Bridge', built 1806 and replaced 1896. ©Highland Photographic Archive

record of their adventures. In *Letters from the North Highlands* during the summer 1816, Elizabeth Isabella Spence provides another perspective of what happened:

'LETTER XXII

Inverness, 14 August, 1816

Oh! My dear friend, what an awful night was the last in Inverness! The earth trembled, the hills shook, and all nature was convulsed.

At midnight this place was visited by an awful shock of an earthquake.

People were thrown from their beds, furniture was overturned, dwellings almost unroofed, chimnies gave way, and the streets exhibited a scene of the most mournful devastation, being strewn with huge masses of stone, hurled from the buildings. The inhabitants, awe-struck, fled from their houses in terror and alarm. The whole people of the town, in a short time, were assembled in the streets, which they paced, men, women, and children, during the most part of the night, afraid to return to their dwellings, and looking with a sort of breathless apprehension for a repetition of the awful visitation of the Almighty.

There was a fearful stillness in the air, such as was described to hover over Lisbon when it was affected in the year 1755. The spectacle exhibited here of apprehension in the countenance of the people,

Crown Cottages, Midmills Road, demolished in 1897 to make way for Crown Church, completed in 1901.
©Highland Photographic Archive

augmented my own terror, when the earth seemed almost ready to open again (from the alarming state of the atmosphere), to swallow us up, so terrible was the deathlike gloom and stillness which prevailed.

The questions and inquiries asked of one another, vain as seemed all hope of satisfaction in the reply, was a melancholy sort of relief, in hearing a human voice, though breathing only the accents of dismay. Persons who had never before spoken to each other, though inhabiting the same place, became in a moment acquainted. One general interest, one general anziety prevailed, while groups of people formed themselves into parties, and fled to the fields during the night, as the safest place of refuge.'

This graphic account gives a real sense of a community in shock and fear, responding to a frightening natural event. It affected Elizabeth Spence deeply. In her next letter she was able to express some of her feelings:

'Never did I quit any place in a more cheerless state of mind than Inverness. The impression of the awful visitation of the former evening so far from having passed away, has left a sensation of apprehension on my spirits, there is no describing. The electric shock sustained at that terrible moment, when the opening of the earth threatened either to swallow one up, or to bury the inhabitants of Inverness in the ruins of the city, by immediate destruction, devastation having spread its calamitous hand in all the neighbourhood, has quite unnerved me. The day, too, has been in perfect unison with myfeelings – lowering, gloomy, and rainy. All the green wooded hills of Inverness were veiled in a heavy mist, which no ray of sunshine attempted to penetrate, gave to the face of a country, wild, mountainous, and uncultured, a depressing aspect, which the stern scenery around this solitary, comfortless inn, does not tend to dispel.'

Elizabeth Spence also describes, in some detail, the costume and dress worn by the inhabitants of Inverness in 1816:

'Some of the old costumes in dress are still preserved; a cap, called a toy, is yet worn, and which in Catholic times must have been the prevailing dress of the country, as it more resembles a nun's hood than any other head-dress to which I can compare it. The toy is made of coarse linen, in front something resembling a mob, with long lappets [loose overlapping folds of fabric], and a kind of tippet [a shawl or wrap] appended to it. The plaid thrown over the head and shoulders I saw worn on Sunday, by a few old women; also the large silver brooch, described by Pennant; but our English habit begins now to be substituted amongst the gayer part of the community, for their own national attire, which looks remarkably picturesque and appropriate to the wild scenery of their country. On Sunday, the inhabitants, young and old, high and low, appear dressed, in respect to the day; and it is a most pleasing object to behold all the children, and young women, walking without caps or bonnets, with their hair nicely braided up; some confined with snods, which is composed of a piece of ribbon or coloured worsted, and is put tight round the head. This marks the distinction between the maiden and the wife, for until a woman is married, in this part of Scotland, she never wears a cap. The elderly men use the Scotch bonnet universally, and are always habited in a suit of light blue cloth, which materials are wove at home. They enwrap themselves in the drapery of the plaid; it looks very graceful, and gives something of the Roman character to their air, which is always stately and erect. Disencumbered in childhood of drapery, the limbs being unfettered, it is rare to see either a lame or ricketty child, or a deformed person. To learn to dance is generally a part of education and this healthful exercise gives an elasticity to the body, which renders the deportment easy. It is thought that the ladies who appear in the streets of Edinburgh, step with more grace, united to modesty, than any women in Europe.'

Elizabeth Spence also brought a sensitive nose to her descriptions of the town in 1816:

'Inverness stands at the foot of a magnificent amphitheatre of hills, so picturesque and diversified in shape, as to form one of the finest natural landscapes it is possible to imagine.

Inverness is the capital of the Highlands, and considered the only town, north of Aberdeen, of importance. It is large and populous but the idea I had formed of noble streets, and elegant houses, greatly disappointed me, on a near approach. Like several of the Scotch towns, which owe their beauty to situation, the charm is lost on entering, from the old and irregular appearance of many of the houses, to which a handsome one often unites; and the quantity of fish hung over the doors of the ordinary dwellings, for the purpose of drying, is very disgusting in warm weather. The squalid dirty aspect of the children, take from all the engaging attraction of infancy. Civilisation in the lower class seems here to be almost a century behind, as far as regards necessary comfort; this is the more extraordinary, as there is such a striking superiority of refinement, in language, and courtesy of manner, in the inhabitants of Inverness, which extends to the humblest individual. English is here universally spoken, and in a state of purity and correctness, which renders it perfectly beautiful. It gives a softness to the manners, extremely graceful, which, united with the Highland urbanity of character, at once win upon a stranger. The Gaelic used, I am told, by all the ordinary people, is very comprehensive and powerful. It seems, to my ear, to have great affinity to the Welch.'

19TH CENTURY
SOCIAL CONDITIONS

ONE OF the most interesting episodes in the social history of Inverness in the first half of the 19th century is the cholera epidemic which swept the Highlands in 1832. Cholera was endemic in the British population at the time and in November 1831 the Town Council called a meeting of Magistrates, Ministers and Medical Practitioners to make plans to combat a possible epidemic in the Highlands. Following advice from Government, recommendations, quoted in the *Inverness Journal* of 11 November 1831, were adopted:

'The inhabitants of the burgh and suburbs should pay the strictest and most scrupulous attention to cleanliness, not only in their houses but on their own persons; and that they should forthwith take the precaution of washing the inner walls of their houses as well as their furniture with a white-wash, composed of quick lime and at all times to allow a free admission of air – and further use the utmost diligence in the immediate removal of all manure and pigstyes from and about their premises and recommending to all butchers in town and neighbourhood, to remove INSTANTLY the offals of the animals slaughtered in their shambles.'.

Some of the serious public health problems in Inverness are obvious from this: overcrowded housing, lack of public sanitation and a woeful public awareness of the dangers of dunghills.

In February 1832 the local Board of Health put in hand plans for a temporary cholera hospital and asked for 'the benevolent' in the town to donate blankets and 'body clothes', in view of 'a large proportion of the poor in the town being in state of great destitution from want of clothing'. Towards the end of the month cholera cases were reported at Fort George and at Stornoway.

By July 1832 cholera was rife in Edinburgh and Leith and cases were reported from Wick and Helmsdale, then from Dingwall and Maryburgh. The Board of Health called another public meeting and gave notice of its intention to take special powers to combat the disease, should it arrive in the burgh. By 10 August the local papers were carrying reports of fatal cases in Dingwall, Wick,

Maryburgh, Portmahomack and Helmsdale. On 17 August fatal cases in Nairn were reported. On 24 August the *Inverness Journal* announced the first cases in Inverness; by the next week there were 112 cases in the town, with already 24 deaths. By 7 September the total number of cases had risen to 211, with 55 deaths 'this disease continues to rage in Inverness with undiminished virulence. It has extended almost to every corner of the town.'

The papers were now publishing distressing stories:

'A Drover who passed through Inverness two days ago was seized with cholera on the evening of the same day at the Muir of Ord. Dr Hall, from Dingwall, was sent for, but medical aid proved unavailing; he expired on Wednesday night, and was interred yesterday. It was with great difficulty that people could be prevailed on to carry the unfortunate man's remains to the grave.

On the same day Murdo Macgregor, Fairburn, fell a prey to cholera and so greatly were the neighbouring tenants in terror of the contagion that the deceased's daughter, who alone of all his relatives remained by his deathbed, had to leave money on a stone at some distance from the house, to purchase linens for his shroud. The linens were procured and deposited in the same place. This man was interred yesterday by his son and son in law in Urray church-yard.' (*Inverness Journal*, 7 September 1832)

By 14 September the epidemic in Inverness had been raging for three weeks:

'THE CHOLERA - We regret to day that this disease, which has prevailed in Inverness for three weeks, has not hitherto lost any of its virulence. In the Merkinch it has been very active and the greatest consternation prevails among the inhabitants; a great portion of them are very destitute both of food and clothing, and reside in dirty lanes and ill ventilated houses, they consequently become predisposed to the pestilency. The deaths since last night are 12, a greater number than

Inverness in the 1850s; drawing by Alexander Mackintosh. ©Highland Photographic Archive

have occurred in the same space of time since its origin here.'
(*Inverness Journal*, 14 September 1832)

The death toll in Inverness now stood at 99, from 302 cases. By the following week the fatalities had risen to 120, from 367 cases, with signs that the intensity of the outbreak was subsiding, though its effects were still felt. Constable William Shaw, who had acted as an attendant at the Cholera Hospital since its establishment, died within 24 hours of exhibiting symptoms. By 28 September there were a total of 136 deaths from 420 cases; by 5 October, 149 deaths from 456 cases. By 12 October the disease had been active for seven weeks, with 154 deaths from 490 cases, but the end seemed to be in sight. In the *Inverness Journal* of 19 October the total cases were listed as 513, with 161 deaths; by 26 October the total had risen to 543, with 168 deaths and 328 recoveries and 47 cases outstanding. By December the outbreak was officially over, with a total of 217 cholera deaths in Inverness since 21 August.

Dr John Inglis Nicol, the medical officer with responsibility for public health in Inverness, contributed this to George Anderson's 1841 *Report on the Sanitary Conditions of the Labouring Classes of Inverness*:

'Inverness is a nice town, situated in a most beautiful country, and with every facility for cleanliness and comfort. The people are, generally speaking, a nice people, but their sufferance of nastiness is past endurance. Contagious fever is seldom or ever absent; but for many years it has seldom been rife in its pestiferous influence. The people owe this more to the kindness of Almighty god than to any means taken or observed for its prevention. There are very few houses in town which can boast of either water-closet or privy; and only two or three public privies in the better part of the place exist for the great bulk of the inhabitants. Hence there is not a street, lane, or approach to it that is not disgustingly defiled at all times, so much so as to render the whole place an absolute nuisance. The *midden* is the chief object of the humble; and though enough of water for purposes of cleanliness may be had by little trouble, still the ablutions are seldom – MUCK in doors and out of doors *must* be their portion. When cholera prevailed in Inverness, it was more fatal than in almost any other town of its population in Britain.'

In 1845 intimations of the Irish potato famine began to reach the Highlands and although government relief efforts were, of necessity, directed mainly at the disastrous situation across in Ireland, it became clear that this catastrophe was going to affect Scotland too. In the summer of 1845 the Inverness papers reported public meetings to organise relief in those parts of the Highlands and Islands that depended on the potato crop. People could see that arrangements for the oncoming winter would need to be made, as no part of the Highlands escaped the potato blight, even on the outskirts of Inverness:

'The mysterious potato disease, which alike baffles all cure and

Photograph of an 1840 sketch of the Post Office, on the corner of Bank Lane and Church Street. ©Highland Photographic Archive

prevention, is fast spreading its ravages over this the and neighbouring counties... Black and withered shaws meet us in various directions, and the tubers, on being taken up, are found to be generally tainted. One gentleman who had a crop of fully £200 value, informs us that though his potatoes appeared sound and healthy on Friday last, they are now wholly gone. In the vicinity of the town – on the banks of the Canal, the fields near the Longman, at Kessock, &c. – the disease is prevalent, and at our market to-day parties were cutting open the potatoes before venturing on purchasing them...

Every day brings intelligence of new failures, and it is feared that the whole potato crop in the north will be destroyed. We have received accounts from Beauly, Fortrose, Glen-Urquhart, Stratherrick, and other districts, where the disease is almost universal. From Fort-Augustus, over the whole West Highlands, the disease prevails, and it is impossible to describe the fears and distress which this wide-spread calamity has occasioned. The Scottish poor and working-classes depend almost as much on the potato crop as the lower Irish. It is their staple, and in many cases their sole food, and unless Indian Corn (maize) or some other substitute be imported, destitution of the severest character will ensue. Steps should also be taken for converting part of the potato crop, ere it is too late, into flour, and the sound part of diseased potatoes into starch. We hope the wealthy and intelligent part of the population will unite to aid their poorer neighbours in mitigating, as far as possible, the effects of this public calamity.' (*Inverness Courier*, 19 August 1846)

Some potatoes were harvested before the blight struck and were stored by landowners with a view to exporting them in due course, when the price had risen sufficiently. The situation came to a head in Inverness early in 1846, when it became known that two vessels lying in Inverness harbour were to be loaded with potatoes for the London market. After initial skirmishes, the situation deteriorated rapidly and the authorities felt that public order was threatened:

'...the supply in the town market for the previous two or three weeks was insufficient, particularly as the poor can only afford to purchase a small supply at a time. These circumstances caused a panic or alarm among a large number of people, which was fomented by some reckless and desperate characters bent on mischief. A mob, composed principally of women and boys, assembled on Tuesday night and turned back the carts on their way to Thornbush Pier. On Wednesday night the shipment was again attempted, in presence of Sheriff-Depute (W. Fraser-Tytler, Esq.), the Provost and Magistrates of the town, the

Balnain House and West Parish Church, 1871. The church was built in 1840. ©Highland Photographic Archive

constables and several Justices of the Peace. The carts were again turned back and the local authorities not only deforced but assaulted. As it was obvious that the civil power could not preserve the peace, a despatch was sent for a party of the 87th regiment, stationed at Fort George and the same night 70 men, under the command of Captain Campbell, arrived and took up their quarters in the castle. Thursday being a fast-day, preparatory to the usual sacramental solemnity, it was resolved to desist from any further display of authority till the following day, and in the meantime the subjoined proclamation was issued:-

"Proclamation by the Provost and Magistrates of Inverness

Whereas numbers of disorderly persons have unlawfully prevented the shipment of potatoes on board two vessels now at Inverness, the Provost and Magistrates hereby intimate, that the crop of potatoes in the north of Scotland has this season been larger than usual, that in other places it has been defective; that it is unjust as well as illegal, to endeavour to prevent the surplus in this quarter from being sent to supply, in part, the deficiency elsewhere; that the civil power, aided by the military from Fort George, now in this town, are ready to preserve the peace and to enforce order...

By order of the Provost and Magistrates of Inverness.

ALEX MACTAVISH, Town-clerk

Inverness 4 February 1846"

Notwithstanding this warning... the populace assembled in the evening to the number of fully 1500... About 50 or 60 of the mob carried large sticks or palings, which they shouldered like muskets... and then proceeded up the Haugh, where they broke some of the windows in Dr Nicol's house. Their next progress was to Telford Street, where Provost Sutherland resides. An attack was made on the Provost's house... The house of Mr Masson, steamboat agent, was

View of Inverness, 1840s, showing the bridge destroyed in the flood of 1849. ©Highland Photographic Archive

treated in the same manner, and the mob next threatened to proceed to Petty Street... The extent and violence of these outrages, and the object of the crowd being the destruction of property, it was judged necessary to call out the military to protect the town. This was accordingly done and about 20 of the rioters secured...

On Friday morning, 200 of the principal inhabitants were summoned by the Provost to the Town Hall, and sworn in as special constables... At the same time it was felt to be necessary to vindicate the authority of the law and repress the tendency towards insubordination. One cart of potatoes was brought to the High Street, and the civil power again formed an escort to proceed with it to the pier. At this time the streets were thronged with a dense assemblage of the lower classes of the people, including a great number of woman... the civil procession, had without molestation, gone as far as Waterloo Place, when the Provost was struck with a stone. Sheriff Tytler then read the Riot Act, after which the party continued on their way to the pier... and when the cart reached the pier the mob must have consisted of 5000 persons. It was found impossible to ship the potatoes. The mob seized on the cart, and with sticks and stones drove off the constables. Large stones were thrown at the party, some of whom were cut and seriously injured... The party took refuge in Mr Loban's brewery-yard, having previously dispatched a man on horse back for the military, and the mob then emptied the potatoes on the pier... and threw the cart into the river, amidst vociferous cheering... The soldiers, however, were received with groans and hootings, and some stones were thrown at them... After a short time peace was restored, and the detachment was marched back to the castle.

On Saturday eight cart loads of potatoes were conveyed to the vessel, escorted by the military, and were put on board without any attempt at disturbance.' (*Inverness Courier*, 11 February 1846)

Similar disturbances, primarily involving grain speculation, took place in other towns and villages in the Highlands, reaching a peak in February 1847, though there was nothing quite so serious again in Inverness. The Highland Destitution Board, formed to organise a public response to the emergency, organised the distribution of food aid until the crisis was brought under control with a good harvest in 1849.

Much research remains to be done into the detail of social conditions in Inverness in this crucial period of the 19th century. The response by public authorities to the potato famine did much to inform the public response in later years to the crises of emigrations and clearances which endangered the economy and social fabric of the Highlands. Public opinion was shaped by Inverness newspaper editors, on all sides, from the most radical to the most conservative, but only a detailed study of the newspapers of the period can unravel the complexities of why public policy evolved as it did. In particular, it is only in the newspapers, or sometimes in court records, that what the editor of the *Inverness Courier* in 1846 identified as 'the lower orders' find their voice, even when that voice is recorded so unsympathetically.

The 1840s brought two other events of note which were to have far-reaching effects on social conditions in Inverness. This was a period in Highland history when the politics of religion was far more important to the vast majority of the population than the politics of state. Reams could be written on the way religious controversies played out in the Highland capital in the 1840s, culminating in the great split down the middle of Presbyterianism in 1843 that is known as the

Boys in Inverness Indoor Market, 1870. ©Highland Photographic Archive

Parade of Inverness Volunteers at Farraline Park, 1895. Bell's Institution was built in 1841. It became a courthouse in 1937 and has housed the public library since 1980. ©Highland Photographic Archive

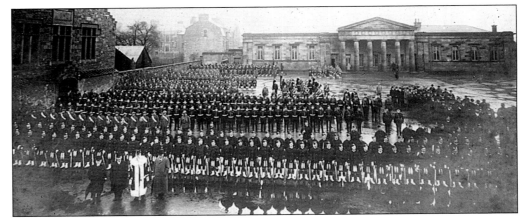

Disruption. This is not the place to deal with the substance of the dispute, except to say that it was at its root an argument over the issue of patronage – put simplistically, whether a congregation or a landlord had the legal authority to appoint a parish minister. The issue split all Highland communities and even families, right down the middle and was perhaps the major factor in generating a tremendous interest in religious matters throughout the last half of the 19th century. Church membership soared and the disruptionists – the Free Church of Scotland as they became known – ploughed the fruits of mid-Victorian prosperity into impressive new church buildings. Today we live with this architectural legacy, in an age in which church membership is but a fraction of what it was in the 19th century, which is why so many ecclesiastical premises in Inverness are now used for non-religious purposes.

The other national event which affected Inverness in the 1840s and thereafter was the inauguration of a decennial national enumerated Census in 1841, which counted all the inhabitants in each parish, with details of their ages, occupations, addresses, households, places of birth and even their ability to speak Gaelic. At the time the results were collated and released as statistical totals which could be used as accurate gauges of population trends. Today, of course, we have access to the enumerator's notebooks, giving the detail much beloved of ancestor hunters. However, the amount of social detail which lies unexploited in the Censuses is phenomenal, with only a tiny amount of research so far undertaken into what they have to tell us about social conditions in Inverness. The Census provides a snapshot of Inverness society every ten years and is now available up to and including that of 1901 – for reasons of confidentiality the next Census, that of 1911, will not be released to social researchers and genealogists until 2011.

The Reform Bill of 1832 brought intimations of political and electoral reform which would eventually outdo the wildest dreams of those who sought to widen the franchise, so that by the end of the century the political and social landscape of the Highlands would be completely transformed. Queen Victoria ascended to the throne in 1837; the Victorian Age in the Highlands brought many changes, not just in social conditions but to the urban landscape of Inverness, largely as a result of the transformation of the commercial centre of the town after the coming of the railway.

THE RAILWAY AGE

T HE COMING of the railway to Inverness was to have enormous social and economic effects on the development of the town, but this was not realised immediately by everybody. The railway came to Inverness gradually, in stages, so perhaps the dramatic effect was disguised somewhat to those who lived through years of frustration as different schemes were floated.

The railway from Perth to Aberdeen was completed in 1850 and soon the Great North of Scotland Railway was building westward, towards Elgin and Nairn. Meanwhile the Inverness and Nairn railway opened in 1855. The connection to Inverness was completed on 11 October 1858, making a direct rail link from Inverness to the south a possibility at long last.

Lochgorm locomotive works, built 1864, included machine shops, erecting shop, paint room and a roundhouse with a massive turntable.
©Highland Photographic Archive

Drawing by Alexander Mackintosh of the Raigmore, *the first steam engine built specially for the Highland Railway Co.* ©Highland Photographic Archive

Forbes Fountain, High Street, 1880. ©Highland Photographic Archive

Well, not quite. Passengers still had to negotiate in Aberdeen a distance of over half a mile from the Waterloo station, at which the train from Inverness arrived, to the Guild Street station, from which trains for the south departed. With two separate railway companies, whose Directors found cooperation impossible, customer satisfaction was not a high priority. This often meant an overnight stay in Aberdeen, especially for passengers travelling from the south.

This unsatisfactory state of affairs was the subject of much investigation in Inverness. Joseph Mitchell, the famous railway engineer who made his home in Inverness and whose *Reminiscences of My Life in the Highlands* is a useful and informative source for this period, had planned a direct route from Inverness to Perth as early as 1845.

Meanwhile, the railway northward from Perth was under construction, reaching Dunkeld in 1856. By 1860 Joseph Mitchell was surveying a route from Dunkeld to Grantown and on to Forres and soon the Inverness and Perth Junction Railway was applying to Parliament for an Act to enable this route to be developed. The 13 miles from Dunkeld to Pitlochry were opened on 1 June

*Inverness in the 1890s.
©Highland Photographic
Archive*

1863. The 36 miles from Forres to Aviemore opened on 3 August and the final link of 55 miles from Aviemore to Pitlochry, through the Drumochter Pass, was completed on 9 September – an impressive feat of construction engineering. The Highland Railway was complete at last. The timetable promised a 'Great Saving of Time and Money in Travelling to and from the North of Scotland'. Newspaper advertising promised journey times of six hours from Inverness to Perth, eight and a half hours to Glasgow or Edinburgh and 18 hours to London. By contrast, the mail coach from Inverness to Perth at this time took 14 hours.

However, detailed examination of the printed timetable revealed not quite so optimistic a prospect for travellers. This shows that the train leaving Inverness at 9am reached Forres at 10.15am. Here it was merged with a train which had left Keith at 8.30am. At 10.25am it set off for Perth, arriving there at 3.30pm and reaching Glasgow at 6.15pm, or over nine hours after leaving Inverness. Passengers continuing to London would reach Euston station at 4.37am the following morning – just short of 20 hours from Inverness.

An 'Express' train left Inverness daily at 1.05pm, arriving in Perth at 7pm and at Glasgow at 9.45pm, reaching London at 9.40am the following morning – 20½ hours after leaving Inverness. Today's direct GNER trains take a little over eight hours. There were no toilet facilities and no catering, on 19th-century trains, so a mad dash for station facilities was a common occurrence.

Needless to say, the intention of the railway company to run trains on a Sunday did not meet with approval from the Free Church Presbytery, who registered their objection.

The railway companies took themselves very seriously and issued Regulations for their customers, who were of course initially unfamiliar with this new mode of travel. Attempting to leave or to board a moving train was strictly forbidden and led to occasional prosecutions. On 21 June 1864 the *Inverness Courier* reported an unusual instance of a breach of railway regulations:

'LEAPING FROM A RAILWAY TRAIN

Upon Tuesday last, as the 7.50pm train left the Tillynaught Junction for Banff, and when about 200 to 300 yards from the station, a prisoner, who was in custody of an officer, leaped from the train tumbling head foremost. The officer leaped after him, and fell two or three times before he could regain his feet properly. A grand chase then took place, but the officer retook his man about a mile from the station. Both were, however, surprised to find themselves made prisoners by the railway officials who came up at the same moment, accusing them of breach of the Company's rules in leaping from a train in motion. The tables were, however, turned when the officer explained the nature of the case and called upon the station agent in Her Majesty's name and authority, to assist him in taking his prisoner back to the station, which he did, as he was bound to do. The station agent reported the case, and the prisoner, who is a civil debtor, will no doubt be tried for breach of the Company's bye-laws.'

Rose Street signal box.
©Highland Photographic
Archive

The first passenger carriages bought by the Inverness and Nairn Railway Company for its opening in 1855 were quite basic. The third-class carriages had four compartments, each seating ten people. First-class carriages were understandably more commodious, with three compartments each seating eight people. Third-class passengers sat on plain wooden seats while in first-class there were padded seats. In the early years there was no heating, but rugs and pillows could be hired for the journey.

Awareness of the needs of passengers produced gradual improvements, with heating introduced (at least for first-class passengers) in the early 1900s and refreshment facilities and dining cars by the 1920s. A new bookstall was opened at Inverness railway station in 1896 as the *Scottish Highlander* of 14 May 1896 proclaimed:

'IMPROVEMENT AT INVERNESS RAILWAY STATION

Steam train passing Seafield, on the outskirts of Inverness. ©Highland Photographic Archive

A welcome improvement is in course of being effected at the Inverness Railway Station, or rather in connection with one of the pertinents of the station, namely, the bookstall. For a long time past it was only too apparent that the accommodation afforded by the existing bookstall was out of all proportion to the amount of business transacted. Not so, however, with its successor. Ample, accommodation, an important desideratum when the clamant demands of the impatient railway traveller have to be attended to, is provided, while from an artistic point of view it is all that could be desired. Erected of pitch pine wood, and of ornate design, the new bookstall, as has been said, is a welcome improvement for which Messrs Menzies deserve credit.'

Clearly the diversion through Forres made the journey south unacceptably long for northern passengers and the railway company soon began to investigate a direct link from Inverness to Aviemore over the Slochd, through Daviot, Moy and Carrbridge, cutting 26 miles off the original line. This difficult route was completed in stages and finally opened on 1 November 1898. Apart from improved journey times for passengers, one of the main motivations for this effort was a threat from the West Highland railway company to build a line up the Great Glen to Inverness, threatening the Highland Railway's monopoly. One of the stops was Culloden Moor Station, described as 'a large and ornate structure which has all the necessary conveniences for those who visit this historical ground' – the battlefield was less than a mile to the west.

The Nairn Viaduct, crossing the river Nairn at Clava, was a monumental feat of engineering – 1785 feet long, with 28 arches, at a height of 140 feet above the river. Each arch with a span of 50 feet, except for the 100-foot long arch spanning the river. This impressive structure is built of red sandstone. Almost as impressive was the Findhorn Viaduct – 1335 feet long, 140 feet high, made up of nine arches with a 36 foot span, with a graceful curve of a half-mile radius.

The line from Aviemore to Forres was axed by Dr Beeching in 1965, with goods trains continuing until 1969. The Strathspey steam preservation railway opened five miles of track, from Aviemore to Boat of Garten, in 1978, with plans to extend to Grantown.

Inverness was not well prepared for the railway age, lacking both the infrastructure to support the influx of passengers – especially summer tourists – and the vision to realise its economic potential. Gradually the infrastructure was provided – hotels, excursions, shops – and a few entrepreneurs seized the opportunities for the development of the town centre, preparing the way for commercial growth with increased facilities and space for shops and offices. Foremost amongst these was local lawyer and politician Charles Fraser Mackintosh, with his friends and business partners. In an obituary published in the *Inverness Courier* on 29 January 1901, the importance of his vision is recognised:

'In the early [18] sixties Mr Fraser Mackintosh and a few other citizens
conceived the idea of opening up a thoroughfare through the network
of back tenements which then lay between the Caledonian Hotel and
the Railway Station entrance. With infinite patience the necessary
properties were one by one bought up, and 1863 found the face of
Inverness transformed by the opening up of what remains to this day
its most handsome thoroughfare – Union Street. In the year in which
Union Street was completed Mr Fraser Mackintosh purchased the
beautiful estate of Drummond, which had belonged many years before
to his great-great-uncle, Provost Phineas Mackintosh. The estate was
immediately opened up for feuing purposes (subdividing into
individual property units) – the first land in the neighbourhood of
Inverness which was made available for that purpose. The example
thus set was speedily followed by other proprietors, and it is not more
than the bare truth that modern Inverness takes its date from the
purchase of Drummond estate. In the following year Ballifeary was
purchased and opened up in the same way.'.

The redevelopment of Union Street, Queensgate, Church Street, High Street
and Academy Street laid the foundations for the townscape we see today,
sweeping away all that remained of mediaeval and 18th-century Inverness. Some
of these impressive Victorian buildings, in their turn, were demolished in the
1960s in another fever of redevelopment, but while the architectural vandalism
was comparable the results were not so impressive.

Railway excursions were a feature of the summer months, often arranged by

the railway company in conjunction with annual events such as agricultural shows, or on public holidays when special trains were run, for example to the beach at Nairn. The summer of 1876 produced a spell of sunny, settled weather in June and, on a Saturday at the end of the month, the Highland Railway treated its workmen, together with their wives and friends, to their annual excursion to Aberdeen, as described in the *Inverness Courier* for 29 June 1876:

> 'The train, which conveyed upwards of 900 passengers, left Inverness at 5 am, and returned at a little after 11 at night. The excursionists were accompanied with the band of the Artillery volunteers, who preceded them to the Aberdeen Drill Hall, where various games were engaged in to the satisfaction and enjoyment of old and young. On the whole, a very pleasant day was passed.'

Why 'on the whole?' Certainly one can imagine that the journey home, at the end of such a very long day, might have detracted from the enjoyment of the experience, with tired, fractious children and just perhaps the odd railwayman slightly the worse for wear after a day out in the big city.

The process was reciprocal: the same newspaper report mentions that 'on Monday, a party of 435 excursionists from Dundee came over the Highland line' for a day out in Inverness.

It is impossible to exaggerate the importance of the coming of the railway to the economic development of Inverness. Prior to the railway, most freight came into Inverness by sea – the road system through the Highlands was not up to the demands of industrial and economic expansion. The introduction of railways to the Highlands was not without its problems. In the construction phase, it brought thousands of 'navvies' to unsuspecting rural villages. They worked hard and drank harder and their exploits often entertained the court reporters of local newspapers.

Railways had a more permanent effect on some Highland villages, forcing them to develop around the railway station, which sometimes, as at Aviemore, was some distance from the traditional settlement site. The impact of tourism was not anticipated at first, but soon communities responded to the need, as market forces prevailed. Nairn became a boom town for tourism, with economically beneficial results; the benefits for Aviemore were much more dubious, especially in the tourist architecture of the 20th century.

Railways opened up to the outside world communities which up til then had seemed impossibly remote. Travel to these 'romantic' locations was, in the 18th century, the prerogative of the wealthy. With the advent of railways it became possible for the masses. It is ironic that with the decline of the railway network in recent years the tourist industry has become, once again, the mainstay of small Highland communities.

Much research has been done on railways in the Highlands. Apart from the writings of Joseph Mitchell, particular acknowledgment is due to Eileen MacAskill and her colleagues in the School Library service, who in the 1980s produced a series of books reproducing newspaper and other source materials; this work was called the Highland Environmental Link Project and the books were produced under a Community Programme contract with the Manpower Services Commission. The Highland Railway Society, through its magazine, is another useful source for operational details of Highland railways.

1890s view of castle and bridge. The bridge was opened in 1855. ©Highland Photographic Archive

LATE VICTORIAN INVERNESS

T HE DEATH of Queen Victoria on 22 January, 1901 marked, for the people of Inverness perhaps more than the rest of Britain, the end of an era. Late January and early February 1901 saw the people of Inverness in mourning for, not just the monarch, but for two of the Highland's most revered characters. In addition to the contemporary death of Dr Alexander Stewart, who wrote under the pen-name 'Nether Lochaber', Invernessians had learned of the death of Charles Fraser Mackintosh on 25 January.

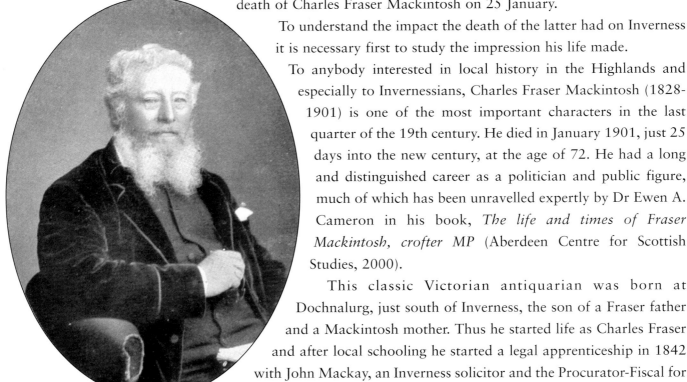

Revd Alexander Stewart, from Loyal Lochaber *by W. Drummond Norie, 1898.*

To understand the impact the death of the latter had on Inverness it is necessary first to study the impression his life made.

To anybody interested in local history in the Highlands and especially to Invernessians, Charles Fraser Mackintosh (1828-1901) is one of the most important characters in the last quarter of the 19th century. He died in January 1901, just 25 days into the new century, at the age of 72. He had a long and distinguished career as a politician and public figure, much of which has been unravelled expertly by Dr Ewen A. Cameron in his book, *The life and times of Fraser Mackintosh, crofter MP* (Aberdeen Centre for Scottish Studies, 2000).

This classic Victorian antiquarian was born at Dochnalurg, just south of Inverness, the son of a Fraser father and a Mackintosh mother. Thus he started life as Charles Fraser and after local schooling he started a legal apprenticeship in 1842 with John Mackay, an Inverness solicitor and the Procurator-Fiscal for the town. After further study at the University of Edinburgh he worked in the legal profession in Inverness from 1849 to 1862, at which point, presumably suitably enriched from his legal practice, he retired at the age of 39.

The reason for his change of name was partly nostalgic but perhaps mostly pecuniary. His uncle Aeneas Mackintosh of Towerside, Forres, died in 1857; in his will he asked Charles Fraser to adopt the Mackintosh surname to prevent that branch of the family dying out. The will stipulated that Charles Fraser Mackintosh could then be regarded as a beneficiary. As a dedicated Jacobite, Charles was pleased to oblige.

In 1863 Charles Fraser Mackintosh had bought the Drummond Estate, which was immediately laid out for feuing. He also was involved in a consortium with G. G. Mackay, D. Davidson and Hugh Rose to redevelop Union Street – they were amongst the first to realise the potential of the railway for the future prosperity of the town centre.

In 1868, recently retired from public life and work, unattached and relatively well off, Mackintosh set out to explore Europe. He was at Malaga in the south of Spain when he received a request from his clan chief, Mackintosh of Mackintosh, inviting him to become his Commissioner (estate factor). He performed this role for five years, overseeing a programme of improvements on the estate, until in 1873 he acceded to a public petition from over 600 electors and agreed to stand for Parliament in the Inverness Burghs constituency. This covered the towns of Inverness, Nairn, Fortrose and Forres – there was a separate parliamentary constituency covering the County of Inverness. In the election of January 1874 he defeated Sir Alexander Matheson by a majority of 255.

This initiated a period of political service which lasted for 18 years. Throughout his career as an MP he was the only Gaelic-speaking member of the House of Commons and took it upon himself to represent the interest of Highland constituents forcefully, especially in the area of crofting reform. In 1878 the great 'Celtic Demonstration' in Inverness gave an indication of public support for reform and in 1883 Mackintosh served as a member of the Napier Commission, the Royal Commission for the Highlands and Islands which took extensive evidence and resulted in the Crofters Act of 1886 which guaranteed security of tenure for crofters.

In his personal life, Mackintosh found the time to get married in the summer of 1875 to Eveline May, only child of Mr Richard David Holland of Brookville, Surrey and Kilvean, Inverness. In 1876 they built Lochardil House (now a hotel) as a family home. There were, however, no children.

By this time Mackintosh had also embarked on a parallel career as an antiquarian and writer, with *Antiquarian Notes: a series of papers regarding families and places in the Highlands*. These essays first appeared in the columns of the *Inverness Advertiser* in 1863 and were published in book form in 1865 in

PLAN.
of the Town of
INVERNESS.

2. *The River Ness*
3. *Kirk Street*
4. *Bridge Street*
5. *East Street*

6. *Castle Street*
7. *The Castle*
8. *The Market Cross*
9. *The Town House*
10. *The Talbooth or County Goal*

E. Garden Sculp.

Plan of Inverness, from Burt's Letters.

Palace Hotel, 1933. The hotel opened in 1890. ©Highland Photographic Archive

a volume which is still much in use today in Inverness Library. He followed this up in 1866 with *Dunachton Past and Present: episodes in the history of the Mackintoshes* and in 1875 with *Invernessiana: a contribution toward a history of the town and parish of Inverness, from 1160 to 1599.*

These works set the tone for all his future output, which was considerable. Charles Fraser Mackintosh was a magpie, collecting together interesting bits and pieces of local and family history which caught his eye. He was a good lawyer, a brilliant politician, an excellent antiquarian and we are grateful to him for his efforts, while wishing that he had been a bit more careful with his source material.

He was at the height of his political career in the 1880s, following his work on the Napier Commission. In the general election of 1885 he defeated two Highland chieftains, Sir Kenneth Mackenzie and Reginald Macleod of Macleod to become the MP for the County of Inverness. He was elected as an Independent Liberal, supporting female suffrage, the nationalisation of railways and the redistribution of large farms among crofters. However, he opposed Irish Home Rule and parted from Gladstone on this issue, changing from an Independent

*Town House, 1958
(built 1878-82).
©Highland
Photographic
Archive*

*Inverness gas works at Manse Place in the 1960s.
Gas was introduced in 1826 by the Inverness
Water and Gas Company; the Town Council took
control in 1875. ©Highland Photographic Archive*

Royal Hotel (now Clydesdale Bank) from Station Square. ©Highland Photographic Archive

Kessock Ferry, 1896.©Highland Photographic Archive

Charles Fraser Mackintosh.

Liberal to a Liberal Unionist. He thus lost the support of the Highland Land League and, in July 1892, was defeated. By this time his health was in decline and he was happy to retire altogether from public life, with homes at Lochardil, Bournemouth and London. In 1893 the *Celtic Monthly* paid tribute to his long career of public service, noting in passing that he was 'a leading member of almost every association which has for its main object the social or educational advancement of the Highland people.'.

These included the Gaelic Societies of Inverness, London and Glasgow. His contributions were recognised by many and he was awarded an honourary LL.D from the University of Aberdeen in 1897.

As a man of some wealth, Mackintosh was able to get some of his political utterances privately printed – the equivalent nowadays, perhaps, of having your own website. He gathered together a collection of materials on the great Reform Demonstration of 1884, including his ticket for the Platform Party, the text of a poem specially written for the occasion, entitled *The March to Lochardil*, a poster advertising the event, with a fine view of the Inverness suspension bridge and newspaper cuttings. He also kept copies of election cartoons and election posters and had those assembled together in specially-made portfolios. Some of the issues, for example the public ownership of railways, are still under discussion today, over a century later.

Charles Fraser Mackintosh was an obsessive and persistent clipper of newspaper articles for all his life. These he collected together and bound in 90 volumes – from the 1850s right up until a few months before his death. He entitled them *Res Septentrionibus* – 'Northern Things' . There is a separate volume of clippings relating to the adventures of the Napier Commission and several volumes of what are effectively scrap books of his European travels in 1872.

Mackintosh found the time in the 1890s to pursue his antiquarian interests. One particularly eclectic production was *Letters of two centuries: chiefly connected with Inverness and the Highlands, from 1616 to 1815.* First published in the *Scottish Highlander* newspaper, these pieces consisted of a letter written in each year of the two centuries, with commentaries and observations. Another compilation of documents was *The last Macdonalds of Isla: chiefly selected from original bonds and documents belonging to Sir James MacDonald, the last of his race, by then in the possession of Charles Fraser-Mackintosh.* This was first

Market Day in Inglis Street, 1890s. ©Highland Photographic Archive

Market Day in Inglis Street, 1890s. ©Highland Photographic Archive

published as papers in the *Celtic Monthly* and then in book form in 1895. Of more interest locally was another volume of local historical essays, *Antiquarian notes, historical genealogical and social, 2nd series: Inverness-shire parish by parish* (1897), first published in the *Scottish Highlander*. After his death this was reissued as a second edition in 1913, with a life of the author and an appendix on the church history of Inverness by Kenneth Macdonald.

In January 1901 Charles Fraser Mackintosh died at his home in Bournemouth and was buried at Kensal Green cemetery in London. He was 72. His widow died in 1921, at which point his personal library of over 5000 volumes was left to Inverness Public Library, where they still reside, forming the core of their collections of books on Highland history, language and culture.

St Andrew's Cathedral (1869); the architect was Alexander Ross. ©Highland Photographic Archive

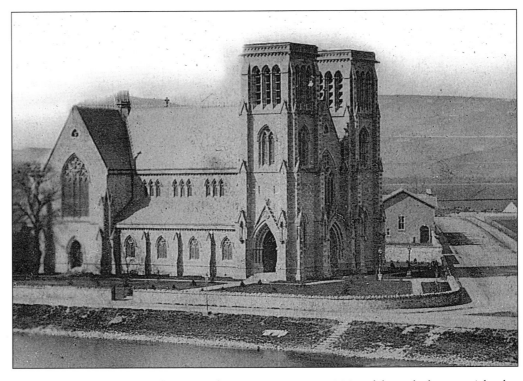

This was a fitting bequest for, on 16 June 1883, although busy with the business of the Napier Commission, Charles Fraser Mackintosh had delivered the main speech on the occasion of the opening of Inverness Free Library. He had campaigned vigorously for the adoption of the Library Act in Inverness – in 1877 – and had assisted with the fundraising which made the initial library possible. He was totally committed to education and learning for the Highland population,

MacPhail, chaplain to the Poorhouse (built 1859-61); later known as Muirfield Institution and then part of Hilton Hospital, now converted into flats. ©Highland Photographic Archive

making this crystal clear in the course of a long speech: 'The main object in view in establishing Free Libraries is, in the first place, the enlightenment and instruction of the people.'

A presentation copy of the first printed catalogue of the book stock of Inverness Free Library, incorporating the stock of the old Burgh Library, was presented to Charles Fraser Mackintosh on the occasion of the opening.
A long obituary appeared in the *Inverness Courier* of 29 January, accompanied by the following appreciation:

> 'The Reaper plies his fatal sickle regardless of the march of centuries, and, ere the first month of 1901 has sped to its close, we have to record, with deep regret, the loss of one who can ill be spared from the fast-diminishing little band of true Highlanders whose first thought and aim were the welfare and progress of their own race. Dr Charles Fraser Mackintosh of Drummond is no more.'

Although there were several obituaries in the Inverness papers after his death, there was perhaps not as much subsequent coverage as he deserved, thanks in part to the deaths of Queen Victoria and Dr Stewart. Nevertheless, the first weeks of the new century left the people of the Highlands in mourning for three people they had loved dearly. It was truly the end of an era.

Jock, resident of The Maggot. ©Highland Photographic Archive

£1 banknote of the Caledonian Banking Co, 1839. The bank was founded in 1838 and had 20 branches by 1845. Its impressive head office in High Street was built in 1847. ©Highland Photographic Archive

At the other end of the social scale, away from public dinners and public events, are the ordinary folk of Inverness who, apart from their occasional appearances in the pages of the local press, pass unseen.

However, these occasional glimpses eventually allow us to build up a fairly complete picture of ordinary and in some cases extraordinary, life in late

Mr Waterson, bank manager.
©Highland Photographic
Archive

Dr Jane Watson, his wife.
©Highland Photographic
Archive

Victorian Inverness. With literally thousands of examples to select from, it seems invidious to pick on one, but a case which caught the public imagination in the autumn of 1882 was the case of 'the baby in the biscuit box', which led to the conviction of Margaret Matheson on charges of child desertion.

The case first hit the local press at the end of August. As described in the *Northern Chronicle* of 30 August, a woman approached a porter at the railway station in Ardersier around six o'clock on a Monday evening and handed him a box, with sixpence to pay for its delivery to a nearby farm. There was nothing at all unusual in this request, so the porter took the box, apparently of biscuits from Mitchell & Muill, Aberdeen and handed it to the mail-gig driver, Mr Cameron, for onward delivery. It was addressed to 'Mrs Macbain' at the farm of Milton of Connage.

The farmer, Mr Malcolm Macbain accepted delivery of the parcel two hours later with some surprise, as his wife had died two years previously. The mail-gig driver mentioned that he had heard sounds 'resembling the mewing of a young cat' emanating from the box. The box was opened: inside was 'a young female child,' an infant. The local doctor and the local policeman were called:

> 'On their arrival, the child was removed from its novel habitation, and taken into care by a wet nurse, under whose care it speedily showed signs of health. While it was being nursed, a letter dropped from its dress, written, evidently, by a woman, and signed in a woman's name.'

The letter, signed by 'Kate Murdoch,' stated that she had been employed at the farm some seven years before and asked, 'for old acquaintance sake,' for the baby to be looked after, promising a financial reward. Nobody at the farm could remember anybody of that name ever working there. The authorities in Inverness were notified and that very night the Chief Constable and the Depute Fiscal arrived to check out this strange discovery. By this time the woman had disappeared.

Subsequent police enquires established that a child had been born in Nairn only five days before the delivery of the biscuit box to Milton farm. The mother was traced to Evanton, in Ross-shire, where Margaret Matheson was apprehended and brought to Inverness in police custody. It was established that she had once worked as a farm servant for Mr Macbain. She was charged, it was reported in the *Inverness Advertiser* of 5 September, of 'deserting and exposing the child to the danger of life.'

The baby was discovered at 6pm on a Monday night and, with a midnight deadline and a newspaper due to be published on Tuesday, the *Inverness Courier* had a chance to scoop its competitors. Unfortunately their reporter was just in too much of a rush and got the facts wrong. 'SUPPOSED CHILD MURDER' was the headline in the issue of 29 August. Unaccountably, in reporting the arrest of a woman, the *Courier* identified her as 'Catherine Matheson'.

This case study illustrates very well the need to consult all available sources when researching, especially when local newspapers are concerned. In 1882 there were three newspapers publishing in Inverness and a careful reading of the reports in all of them adds details to the story. The *Courier*, for example, eventually reported that the baby was well dressed and apparently well cared for and that 'there was a little hole in the box, made by pushing out a knot in the wood, to afford it air' – details which would become important mitigating factors at the trial.

In reporting the trial a month later, the *Inverness Courier*, perhaps mindful that it had not exactly covered itself with journalistic glory in its initial reporting, stuck resolutely to the facts of the case in quite a short and restrained court report. Its reporter sets the scene:

> 'Margaret Matheson, a respectably dressed, and rather nice-looking woman, of about 30 years of age, was charged before Sheriff Ivory, at the Inverness Criminal Court on Saturday, with the crime of exposing and deserting a female child, by placing it in a box between Nairn and Fort-George on Monday, the 28th of August last, to the danger of the child's life. Accused, who was defended by Mr Clarke, solicitor, pleaded not guilty. Mr Anderson prosecuted, and nine witnesses were examined.'

It should not, of course, be assumed that the appearance of ordinary people in local newspapers only occurs when they have committed a criminal act. The witnesses in this case all come to life, albeit briefly, as decent folk going about their daily lives in a conscientious and respectable way. The landlady of the boarding house in Nairn, Mrs Elizabeth Macdonald, testified that Margaret Matheson, calling herself 'Mrs Fraser,' had come to lodge with her in the middle of July, claiming that she lived in Inverness where her husband was a joiner, but had come to Nairn for the sea bathing because she suffered from rheumatism. A Nairn midwife, Mrs Ann James or Hendry, testified that she had delivered the infant on Wednesday 23 August. Mrs Macdonald had walked with Margaret Matheson part of the way to the station on the fateful Monday night, with Margaret Matheson carrying the baby in one arm and a box in the other. The baby was dressed in a white gown and a red petticoat.

John Simpson, a porter at Nairn station, remembered Margaret Matheson arriving in July, when she had handed him a box and asked him to keep it until she called for it. He was going to use it for firewood, but on Saturday 26 August she returned and asked if it was still there and that she would be back to collect it on Monday.

Alexander Graham, the guard on the train, opened a door in a third-class carriage for her at Fort George station. He remembered her carrying a box, which

Dr John Mackenzie, Provost of Inverness and member of the Gaelic Society of Inverness. ©Highland Photographic Archive

she said she wanted to deliver to a porter. Donald Clarke, the railway porter, testified to receiving the box. He noticed that above the address was written 'Please send the box at once'. He gave it to John Chisholm, the mail-gig driver. He put the box at his feet and set off for Ardersier. The driver remembered that the wooden box was tied with a strap and string. In a detail missing from the initial reports, he admitted that he and a couple of boys had heard 'a crying' from the box and 'had a peep into the box from the side of the lid'. He claimed to have seen no child, but only some plaid. Instead of immediately doing anything about it himself he summoned his young assistant, John Cameron, with instructions to take it to Milton of Connage immediately.

The farmer, Malcolm S. Macbain and his son John Macbain received the box together. Again, reports in the local press differ in the amount of detail given. The *Courier* talks of the father being cross-examined at great length and admitting that the accused had worked for him between May and November 1881 – 'He acknowledged having been familiar with her.' According to the *Courier*, the defence alleged that Mr Macbain was in fact the father of the child, but this was denied.

The report in the *Inverness Advertiser* of 29 September 1882 gives far more detail of the cross-examination. Malcolm Macbain admitted that in

Unveiling of Flora MacDonald statue at the castle, 1899. ©Highland Photographic Archive

The Cameron Monument, Station Square, commemorating campaigns in Egypt and the Sudan in the 1880s.

Dr Alexander Ross. ©Highland Photographic Archive

Flora MacDonald statue in winter.

A closer view of the Flora MacDonald statue.

February he had received a letter from Margaret Matheson, accusing him of being the father of her child:

> 'He never denied but than he had connection with the prisoner while she was in his service – only once, however, and that day was on Friday the 7th of October.'

He had burned the letter:

> 'She stated in that letter that she was with child to him, but she did not ask him to make any provision for it. She said that she had others that she could put it on.'

For the defence, Mr Clarke gave Mr Macbain quite a hard time. It turned out that he had in fact instructed his Nairn solicitors to give Margaret Matheson some money to keep her quiet, as long as she dropped the accusation that he was the father of her child. Despite his repeated denials, Mr Macbain did not emerge from the case with his reputation undiminished.

Mr Clarke did his best in mitigation, pleading for leniency, but the sheriff, noting that while precautions had been taken to ensure the survival of the infant, at several points in her journey she could have come to serious harm: 'the railway officials, fortunately for her, had taken every care of the box, else the child might have been killed'. The sheriff seemed a little surprised – 'it was perfectly clear that had the railway officials treated the box as in the usual way, the child might have died'. Under the circumstances he felt unable to do less than pass a sentence of 60 days imprisonment.

This sad case caught the public imagination because of its peculiar circumstances, but in the reports of hundreds of much more ordinary crimes there is also much to be learned about the way Victorian society worked. The newspapers make fascinating reading, as local history researchers know to their cost – it is far too easy to be distracted from the task in hand. Newspapers understood their entertainment function, in the days before electronic media and did their best to give their readership their money's worth. Reporters were skilled in shorthand and could give almost verbatim accounts of speeches and court evidence, almost to the point where it is possible to reconstruct exactly what was said.

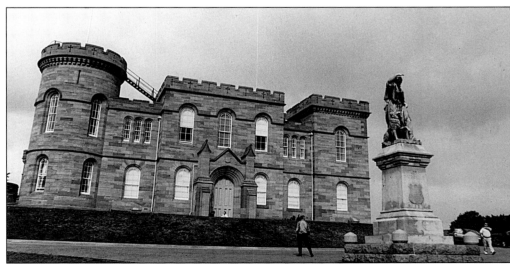

Inverness Castle (Courthouse) and Flora MacDonald statue.

Unveiling of the Cameron Monument in Station Square, 1893, commemorating the campaigns of 1882-5 in Egypt and the Sudan. ©Highland Photographic Archive

Station Square, 1893. The main entrance to the station was designed by Joseph Mitchell and dates from 1855. It was destroyed in the 1960s. The Station Hotel dates from 1859. ©Highland Photographic Archive

INTO A NEW CENTURY

ALMOST unnoticed 1 January 1900 passed, with 'normal' levels of revellers in the streets, but on 1 January 1901 the citizens of Inverness welcomed in the 20th century with some style – it seems, unlike their 21st century peers, the Victorians could count properly and celebrated the turning of the century on the right day. Reports in the local papers described the festivities in much detail. The coverage in the *Highland News* is typical:

'NEW YEAR'S DAY IN INVERNESS

THE STREETS AT MIDNIGHT

The first day of the opening year and beginning of a new century was observed in Inverness as custom and tradition have from time immemorial dictated. The night, although cold, was dry and fairly clear. Long before midnight the streets were well filled, the crowd at the Exchange and along High Street being especially dense.'

Everybody noticed, according to the *Highland News*, that there were more young people than usual out in the streets – particularly quite young children: 'they ran about unattended, and apparently were absolutely untrammelled by any vestige of parental control'.

One senses a high level of irritation in the writer – 'these youngsters largely indulged in fireworks, which they hurled about promiscuously'. Warming to his theme, he goes on to write that the bulk of the crowd 'was as usual composed by young men, who in many cases were accompanied by young women friends'. More intimations of promiscuous behaviour, perhaps?

Unfortunately, as far as the *Highland News* was concerned the public scenes of celebration were marred by drunkenness and loutish behaviour:

'It is regrettable to have to record that there was much drunkenness. On all sides young men – some of them, indeed, mere boys – were seen reeling about in various stages of intoxication. Many of these youths, though, were merely shamming, for by an extraordinary process of reasoning the silly young fellows think that to roll about, to swear and jostle, and, in a word, personate the vulgar 'drunk,' is both manly and correct conduct. Stupidity can go no further, and a drastic, and we

Royal Tartan Warehouse, High Street, decorated for a royal visit. ©Highland Photographic Archive

Inverness spires in 1900: Old High Church, Free North Church (1893), St Columba's High Church (Free High Church, 1852), Town Steeple (1791).

believe effective, method of cure might be found in a lusty application of the parental walking-stick.'

It is not difficult to imagine our intrepid reporter, no doubt the butt of commentary himself, struggling to resist the temptation to set about some of these young reprobates with his own walking stick. He grudgingly admits that while there was far too much horse-play, it was generally of the good-natured variety – this went some way 'to redeem what would otherwise have been utterly discreditable behaviour'.

At last, the hour of transformation arrived:

'The striking of midnight by the Steeple clock was received with an outburst of cheering. Many left almost immediately afterwards, apparently bent on first-footing, but it was hours before the streets were cleared of revellers, and groups of young men, girls, and children were met with until an advanced hour of the morning. So much for the public reception of the new century. The crowd was undoubtedly much larger than usual…'

Several churches held midnight services and the Salvation Army held torchlight processions through the streets – 'and during their progress they were submitted to a great deal of jostling by the mob.'.

There was a large congregation at the Wesleyan Methodist Church, which was decorated with flowers. St John's Episcopal Church and St Mary's Roman Catholic Church were both filled with worshippers. During the day there were services in the Cathedral and in the 'Gaelic Parish Church'. In the Town Hall a special religious service was held to welcome in the new century. After the singing of Psalm 100 the Very Rev Dr Norman Macleod preached on church union, expressing the hope that a larger union of Scottish churches could be accomplished soon, if more Christians 'were to resolve to begin the century with an honest determination to follow the old maxim of live and let live'. This sentiment attracted applause from the assembled company.

Jubilee Celebrations, 22 June 1897. ©Highland Photographic Archive

Jubilee Celebrations, 1897.
©Highland Photographic
Archive

The mild but blustery weather perhaps affected the quality of play at a special football match between Clachnacuddin and the Glasgow football team, Partick Thistle. The 'fairly large' crowd was perhaps due to the early start at noon. Clachnacuddin were three goals up by half time and scored again after the break, whereupon the 'Jags' 'made strenuous efforts to get on an equality' and managed to score three late goals.

At the Poorhouse the inmates enjoyed 'a sumptuous repast' as they were entertained to dinner (at 2pm) at the expense of the Parish Council. 'Several speeches were made' – hopefully the unfortunates did not have to wait too long for their feast. It was noticed as a 'curious fact' that on the occasion of the arrival of the new century there were 100 inmates in the institution. Bailie Sinclair had sent along a large bun for everybody, Mr George Gallon provided apples, while Messrs Macdonald and Mackintosh bestowed 'a supply of oranges' on the inmates.

The soldiers at the Cameron Barracks 'wound up a happy day by holding a successful dance.'

The *Inverness Courier* described events in similar terms – 'a staggering man is a painful sight' – though in not quite such lurid terms as its Temperance competitor:

'THE NEW-YEAR AND THE NEW CENTURY

The weather of New-Year's Day was exceedingly mild, though there were blustering winds and some rains in the early morning. The sun shone brightly and pleasantly during the forenoon and the day continued to be of the genial sort until the evening, when it got somewhat cold. The frost, as Mr Toots might have said, was of no consequence, and the moon shed a fair light. This was all very nice for a day in mid-winter, but it had the inseparable drawback in the muddy state of roads and streets. Many people were afoot, visiting friends and interchanging New-Year greetings, which, for the sake of variety, sometimes took the form of 'A happy new century'. All places of business, save the licensed drinking-places, were closed. These did a lively trade and it could not be doubted that New Year's Day had fully maintained its old, evil reputation for heavy potations. In this matter the new century does not promise to be much better than the old. A great many men, most of them young men, were to be seen under the influence of drink. As good humour was the order of the day the street quarrels were few, and we have not heard that there was any brawl or accident of a serious type. Considering the circumstances that is something to feel thankful for. Special services in commemoration of the opening of the 20th century were held, including one in the Town Hall, which was attended by the Provost, Magistrates and Town Council. In the afternoon amusements were provided, such as football, pantomime and the like. Charitable entertainments were given at the different public institutions, which were decked out in festive fashion with holly, plants, flowers and 'mottoes'. At night the streets were quiet and the people orderly. The new century had arrived and, indeed, had become familiar.'

The *Courier* had even managed to get a shorter report into its Tuesday issue, published as usual even though on New Year's Day. It adds a little more local colour:

'Another unpleasant feature of the lively scene was the too palpable proof of over-indulgence in intoxicating drink. Civil and military police paraded the streets, but we daresay took a more lenient view of their duty than they usually do... All were in good humour, and although the noise and din prevented many from hearing the strokes of the steeple clock, the drum clock in Bridge Street showed that the year and the century had gone, and hands were shaken and greetings for the new year cordially exchanged. The bustle and the fireworks were both kept agoing for some time after midnight, and there were displays of lime-lights at different points, the one at the west end of the Suspension Bridge beautifully illuminating the Castle and the river. Rockets were sent up here and elsewhere.'

The *Northern Chronicle* noted that:

'At Inverness and throughout the Highlands the advent of the 20th century was marked by demonstrations of a character which befitted the unique event.'

It bemoaned the absence of many 'patriots' because of the (Boer) war in South Africa, which was not going well, but, 'still, a new century only comes once in the lifetime of ordinary mortals and the rejoicings were accentuated accordingly'.

There is little coverage of the street scenes, by contrast with both the *Highland News* and the *Inverness Courier*, but extensive reporting of Dr Macleod's sermon at the Town House and of the speeches in the Poorhouse. There is also mention of the crowded performances of the *Bluebeard* pantomime at the Theatre Royal and a very lively sports report of the football match between 'The Thistle' and 'The Clachers' at the Kessock Street ground, in 'soft and slippery' conditions in bright sunlight.

An unexpected side effect of the increased interest in the New Year festivities was the enormous increase of business at the Post Office – letters posted in Inverness were up by 10,000 from the previous year, while parcels were up by 2000, for the week between Christmas Day and New Year's Day

So, Inverness settled down after all the excitement to resume normal life in the new century. Keir Hardie came to Inverness at the invitation of the local branch of the Independent Labour Party and addressed a lively meeting in the Town Hall on the subject of 'The Curse of Militarism'.

The exploits of the Camerons and the Seaforths in South Africa occupy much space in the local newspapers, along with the usual chat and gossip. Then, while memories of all those optimistic predictions for the new century were still fresh in the mind, society was shaken to its very foundations by an event that was unpredictable, though not really unexpected. On Tuesday 22 January 1901 Queen Victoria died, bringing to an end a reign which had commenced in 1837. She was 81 years old and had reigned for over 63 years – for Elizabeth II to equal that record she would have to reign until 2016.

King Edward VII was proclaimed monarch at the Town Cross outside the Town House on Friday 26 January 1901 and many public arrangements were put in hand. Meetings and shinty matches were hastily cancelled or postponed and the whole of Highland society went into mourning. The Sheriff Court was

Gondolier in the Caledonian Canal, introduced 1866, withdrawn 1939 and used as a blockship at Scapa Flow. ©Highland Photographic Archive

adjourned and flags were flown at half-mast throughout the town. Perhaps only the death of Diana, Princess of Wales in 1998 comes close to helping us understand the impact of the death of Queen Victoria.

The coverage of the *Highland News*, in its issue for Saturday 26 January 1901, with its columns separated by thick dark lines, gives a taste of what was involved:

'THE DEATH OF QUEEN VICTORIA
RECEPTION OF THE NEWS IN INVERNESS

The news of the death of Her Majesty reached Inverness shortly after seven pm on Tuesday night and the melancholy tidings were passed from mouth to mouth with the utmost rapidity. The sad intelligence was everywhere received with an unfeigned and heartfelt regret that was personal in its intensity and on all sides were heard tributes to the dead monarch's memory uttered with a sincerity that unmistakeably indicated the high place she had taken in the affections of her subjects. To very many, indeed to the majority of our citizens, the death of the Queen was an event hardly realisable, for during their lives they had known no other monarch than Victoria and her demise felt to them almost like a personal loss. The adverse bulletins published during the day and on Monday had in some measure prepared the public mind for the fatal intelligence, which, when it did come, none the less deeply affected all.

THE CHURCH BELLS

The bells of the High Church, West parish Church, United Free High Church, St Andrew's Cathedral, and the Town Steeple, were tolled, and to many in Inverness this was the first intimation of the death of the Sovereign.'

The editor of the *Inverness Courier* seemed to have struggled a little to find the right words to express the feelings of the community and focussed on her personal attributes rather than on the palpable shock which permeated the community:

'The long and gracious reign of Queen Victoria has come to an end. The Sovereign lady whose character shone with growing lustre throughout so many eventful years has passed from earth to her eternal home. The world moves so rapidly that already, two days after her departure, the sad event seems remote. The Proclamation of the new Sovereign has awakened fresh feelings and interests, and the thoughts of men are gradually turning to the future. But the past cannot be forgotten, and the light of such a life as the Queen lived, placed on a pinnacle of greatness before mankind, will not soon lose its splendour. It will never indeed fade from the memory of the nation, but will remain as one of its most fondly cherished possessions… The character of the Queen has done much to unite the peoples that form the British

Empire. She has made the link of the Crown a real and effective bond, not only among English-speaking races, but among all the races that owned her sway. In Scotland we cannot forget how she understood the people, how she loved them and trusted herself among them, and how she touched their hearts. The Highlands and Highlanders had a peculiarly warm place in her affections... She stood forth as an example of enlightened Christian faith, as one who ruled her own home with love and firmness, who kept her Court pure, who realised the responsibilities of her lofty station, and walked in the fear of God. The manifold blessings of Queen Victoria's reign can hardly yet be computed, but she was loved and honoured in her lifetime, and her name will be remembered with reverence.'

Provost Macbean sent a telegram of condolence to the Secretary of State for Scotland in Whitehall and preparations were made for commemorative services in Inverness and throughout the Highlands. The funeral took place in London on 2 February: Mr T. A. Wilson, General Manager of the Highland Railway, inserted a notice in the local papers to intimate that 'all Trains on the Highland Railway will be Stopped from 2.30pm for Ten Minutes.'.

All the churches held memorial services to coincide with the Queen's funeral, with the Provost, Town Council and civic dignitaries attending the one in the High Church. Nowadays, of course, we would all watch proceedings live on television.

The day of the funeral was observed as a fast day in Inverness and all places of business were closed, including all licensed houses and restaurants, except for the refreshment rooms at the railway station. The *Courier* was pleased to note that 'although there were many people perambulating the streets, good order prevailed'.

Many wore black clothes and many buildings and businesses in the town were draped in black or purple cloth. In private houses the blinds and curtains were drawn. The church services were well attended, with people standing in the aisles. The 'official' service in the High Church was filled to overflowing; there was a prevailing sense of national unity. All of this was fully reported, with thick black columnar lines, in the local press.

It is true that Queen Victoria had a long association with the Highlands, dating from her purchase of Balmoral in 1848 as a Highland bolthole for herself and her consort, Albert. He made a visit to Inverness without his Queen; she made only three visits in the course of her long reign, in the words of the *Highland News*, 'of so brief a nature as to be termed flying ones.'

In September 1847 the Queen was visiting Ardverikie Lodge when Albert received a personal invitation from Mr Evan Baillie of Dochfour House to visit Inverness. The town was 'gaily decorated' and a triumphal arch erected at the end of the old stone bridge, which was soon to be swept away in a flood. Guns were brought from Fort George to the Castle hill and a royal salute fired, while Albert received the freedom of the burgh in the Town House and addressed the populace from the front of the building afterwards before returning to Ardverikie.

Queen Victoria herself first visited the town on 6 September 1872, the first royal visit since Queen Mary (Mary, Queen of Scots) passed through in 1562. The royal train stopped at a specially erected platform at Millburn for ten minutes – just long enough for Provost Mackenzie to present a scroll and for another royal salute to be fired – before steaming off to her destination at Dunrobin. Thousands of people flocked into Inverness for the day. Flags were flying everywhere and there was a banquet in her honour held that evening at the Town House. Similar manifestations took place at Dingwall, Tain and Bonar Bridge, en route to Golspie.

The second visit was on Tuesday 16 September 1873. Queen Victoria had been staying for a week at Inverlochy Castle as a guest of Lord Abinger and sailed from Banavie on the Gondolier. The Queen, by now a widow, wore, we are told, a dark dress with a white straw hat, trimmed with black. Carriages met the royal party at Dochfour. They drove through Inverness 'at a smart pace,' through floral arches, to the station where, after a brief ceremony, the royal train left for Balmoral. The town celebrated with a public holiday and the Town Council adjourned to the Town Hall to toast their monarch.

Queen Victoria's third and final visit to Inverness took place on Wednesday 15 September 1877, when her train passed through the station. She was on her way to Loch Maree for a week's holiday. It was noted that 'the train, though it slowed down considerably, made no stoppage and thus considerably disappointed a large crowd which had gathered near the locomotive works and on Rose Street Bridge.'

It is certainly true that Queen Victoria's love of Balmoral put the Highlands on the social map and must have benefited the Highland economy enormously. In the same issue which reported the funeral arrangements for Queen Victoria, the funeral of Charles Fraser Mackintosh was also recognised, with a long obituary of perhaps one of the finest and most productive public servants ever to emerge from Inverness.

Maggot Green (named after St Margaret), before 1910. ©Highland Photographic Archive

INVERNESS IN WORLD WAR ONE

The War Memorial located at Cavell Gardens, overlooking the Ness, across the river from the Cathedral and Eden Court Theatre, incorporates the following inscription:

'DURING THE WAR
UPWARDS OF 5000 MEN OF THE BURGH
AND PARISH OF INVERNESS
WENT OUT ON ACTIVE SERVICE
AND NOBLY UPHELD THE HONOUR
OF THEIR COUNTRY.
OF THESE GALLANT MEN 717 RETURNED NO MORE.
TO THEIR MEMORY THIS MONUMENT
WAS ERECTED BY A GRATEFUL COMMUNITY
AND UNVEILED ON THE 16TH DEC 1922
BY COLONEL THE MACKINTOSH OF MACKINTOSH
LORD LIEUTENANT OF INVERNESS-SHIRE'

It is difficult today to envisage the effect this conflict had on the local community. This was not, of course, by any means the first time that young Invernessians had died in battle. Post-Culloden, in the aftermath of that military disaster, the British Army was more than willing to enlist Highlanders to the Hanoverian cause. Hundreds died in North America fighting – first the French at Quebec and then the American rebels. Hundreds more died in the Peninsular Wars and at Waterloo and in the military disasters in the Crimea and in Afghanistan. In the numerous imperial adventures of the 19th century many hundreds more died, especially in the Sudan, Egypt and in the Boer War, the Anglo-Boer conflict of 1899-1902 in which Highlanders were slaughtered in hundreds at the Moder River.

Traumatic as these conflicts were, the battle casualties were usually numerically trivial by comparison with the massed battles of World War One and the effect on any one Highland community was comparatively little. The Flanders battles were of a completely different character; mass slaughter on a scale never before witnessed in Europe, though hinted at in the American Civil War in the 1860s. The numbers killed between 1914 and 1918, with subsequent campaigns in Russia, affected every Highland community deeply. Every Highland parish has its own war memorial, with columns of names of the dead from the 'Great War' overwhelming the handful of names added to record the death toll of World War Two. The memorial at Cavell Gardens reveals that about 14 per cent, or around one out of every seven soldiers from Inverness parish did not return.

Given such carnage and that many of the 5,000 soldiers from Inverness were men who enlisted after the outbreak of war, there is a temptation to catalogue once again the battles and military campaigns whose victims ended up on the war memorial. In the early months of the war the moral pressure to enlist was considerable and all fit men between the ages of 19 and 40 were expected to answer the call. An *Inverness Courier* advertisement of 11 June 1915 seeking recruits for the 4th Cameron Highlanders contains the implicit assumption that men were already desperately needed to keep the regiment at full fighting strength, having already suffered severe losses. A minimum height of just 5 feet 2 inches was required.

Not everybody was in a hurry to serve the colours. Especially in rural areas, many men sought exemption from military service because of the nature of their work. Thus, woodcutters on the Lovat estate were granted exemptions because the pit props they were producing were needed for the war effort, while a licensed grocer in Beauly was turned down – 'girls will do as well in shops.'

With such a large number of men signed up for military service, it was the women of Inverness who kept the economy going locally. Of course, just because 5000 male Invernessians were away on military service did not mean that there was a shortage of men in the town – the place was buzzing with soldiers from the Cameron Barracks and from Fort George, as well as naval detachments, eventually including (after 1917) some Americans at their Inverness naval base. There were also important naval bases in the Cromarty Firth, for example at Invergordon, whose ratings would swell the numbers in Inverness dance halls and pubs.

Sometimes the war was brought very close to home, as when *HMS Natal* blew up in the Cromarty Firth on Hogmanay 1914, with the loss of over 300 lives, including some local civilians.

Travel north of Inverness during wartime was permitted only by special permission and all residents of the Burgh of Inverness had to carry a Local Pass issued by the local police, containing the resident's name, address and photograph. Despite some shortages, daily life went on much as before, though women with time on their hands could help the war effort by fundraising, knitting, rolling bandages and even gathering spaghnum moss, which was used effectively in field dressings. Some wartime innovations sound quite disgusting by modern tastes – for example 'Pheasant Margarine', sold in 'dainty half-pound packages'.

The Situations Vacant columns in the local newspapers reflected the need for female workers in a much wider range of jobs than previously, while there were patriotic adverts encouraging women to work in 'male' occupations – driving carriages or working on public transport, for example. Many women also enlisted for war service, as cooks, clerks, waitresses and technical workers, while the Scottish Women's Land Army recruited women as milkers and forestry workers. Waste paper was collected and War Bonds and War Savings Certificates were sold.

Pupils at Merkinch School, in 1918, were treated to the presence of American sailors in the neighbouring field, where they assembled mines and from Muirtown Basin sailed out into the North Sea to mine the waters between Orkney and Norway, effectively blockading the German navy.

Throughout the war, the Inverness newspapers gave their readers detailed coverage of events. Often bizarrely optimistic, there was little indication of the scale of total casualties. It must have been clear, however, from the death notices and lists of wounded and missing from Highland regiments that the slaughter was immense.

Compared to some other parts of the Highlands, Inverness escaped relatively lightly. The villages of Easter Ross, for example, suffered badly. The Inverness papers reported the deaths of men from all over the Highlands and Islands. Looking over them now, the reports in the *Highland News* are particularly poignant, as they are often accompanied by photographs of incredibly young-looking men in uniform.

As World War One ended, the Armistice of 11 November 1918 was celebrated in Inverness as elsewhere in the Kingdom. However, just as the surviving archives of the *Inverness Journal* are missing the issues containing reports of the battle of Waterloo in 1815, those of the *Inverness Courier* are without the reports of the way the ending of World War One was celebrated in the Highlands.

Fortunately there are other sources: the *Highland News* and the *Northern Chronicle*. The report in the *Northern Chronicle* on Wednesday 13 November 1918, headlined 'REJOICINGS IN THE NORTH', deals with celebrations in Inverness, Fortrose, Dingwall, Invergordon and Tain:

'INVERNESS

The signing of the armistice was learned in Inverness on Monday forenoon with heartfelt satisfaction. There was gratitude on every hand at the glorious victory achieved by the Allied Powers and the defeat of the arrogant enemy whose 40 years' preparations for world dominion had been overwhelmingly frustrated. By the ringing of the town and church bells the news quickly spread and the streets soon became lively, all joining with enthusiasm in the celebration of the momentous occasion. Flags quickly appeared on the Town Hall, the Castle, and other public and private buildings. The American Y.M.C.A. rooms had

War Memorial, Cavell Gardens. ©Highland Photographic Archive

a particularly effective display. Young people carrying flags paraded the streets in large numbers, and as the afternoon advanced many of the Rose Street Foundry employees and railway workers had processions around the streets. In the evening the streets were crowded. The American Navy men joined heartily in the rejoicings. During the day an American naval band and the local pipe band played selections in the streets. Yesterday the rejoicings were continued, a holiday being granted to the workmen of the Rose Street Foundry. Effigies of the ex-Kaiser were carried in procession and burned on the Exchange. There was a relaxation in the restriction as to the sale of fireworks and youngsters had a great time in the firing of rockets of various sizes. Young women war workers took an active part in the festivities. Bluejackets and Highland and Colonial soldiers in the town enthusiastically took part in the rejoicings.'

These rejoicings were tinged with sadness for five Highland families whose sons were listed in the 'Highland Roll of Honour' alongside reports of the Armistice. But editorially, the *Northern Chronicle* was in uncompromising mode:

'VICTORY

Victory, full, final, and complete, has crowned the efforts of the Allies.

The long weary night of fear and sorrow and struggle has ended, and a new day has dawned on humanity – a day bright with the promise of freedom and of a living and lasting peace. The darkest hour preceded the dawn. The spring of this year saw our enemies strong and arrogant and confident of their power to defeat the Allies in the field before America could put forward her full strength. And we must confess that there seemed ample grounds for their confidence. But since the armies of the Allies, united under the supreme command of General Foch, took the offensive in the middle of July, there has been no pause in their triumphal progress. Now we see the result in a victory which must rank as the most stupendous military achievement in the world's history. No power ever had to submit to so humiliating terms as those which have been imposed upon Germany. We need not waste any sympathy on our chief enemy, who has been brought so low as the result of vaulting ambition…'

The report continues, 'The rejoicings which have taken place over the victorious conclusion of this long war have been sincere and heartfelt, but without any trace of vindictive feeling against our fallen foe. It is not a characteristic of the British nation to cherish hatred, and though we have had deep occasion for scorn and resentment at the way Germany conducted the war, it cannot be said that these feelings are very conspicuous now that a new Germany is arising on the ruins of the old. The war has involved too much sacrifice on our part, and a people chastened with sorrow and conscious of its strength does not cherish vengeful feelings…

Our armies have fought in every part of the Old World, from Archangel to Kilimanjaro, and from Nieuport to Basra, our flag has flown on every sea, and our achievements are known to all the world.'

The editorial ends with a warning that economically difficult times lay ahead, as the task of reconstruction began.

The *Highland News* focused on this theme, avoiding any mention of Victory: 'RIGHT OR WRONG?

The war is ended. Reconstruction is now the task. Whether Reconstruction will proceed upon right or wrong lines is the question that the country will have to answer at the forthcoming general election.

Among the issues the country will have to confront are: establishing a League of Nations, the abolition of conscription, a national housing program, a national minimum wage, land reform, fiscal reform and home rule for Ireland – and Wales!'

The *Highland News* did not approve of the principle of Coalition Government, even in an emergency situation:

'A Coalition Government is essentially bad. It is almost impossible for any part of its policy to be right. It is itself a compromise and therefore its policy is a compromise. Where such policy is a compromise between two wrong policies the result is wrong. When it is a compromise between right and wrong again the result is wrong.'

The Armistice was marked with services of thanksgiving in all the Inverness churches, though sometimes the sermons came dangerously close to enlisting God in the service of the Allied cause. But in the West Church Rev Maclellan ended with a note of realism:

'The end of the war will not bring us anything like perfect happiness. We shall find against us old besetments and new difficulties which must be faced, and entanglements which will be hard to unravel. The days ahead of us will be anxious days, and even in these days of victory there is much to keep us humble.'

Thanksgiving of a different sort was the subject of a report in the *Inverness Courier* of 29 November, with an account of a dinner and ball at the Northern Meeting rooms in honour of the American Thanksgiving Day holiday on the 28th. The commanding officers of 15 US Navy ships and also of the shore bases were joined by local officials and dignitaries in what seems to have been a very pleasant evening. Provost Donald Macdonald, replying to gracious speeches from the American representatives, acknowledged the contribution of the United States to the outcome of the war and in particular the contribution of the mine-laying operations based in Inverness, which had effectively blockaded the German navy for four years.

He also acknowledged that with the ending of hostilities the American presence in Inverness would be missed both by local shopkeepers and by the local girls, leaving some broken hearts behind as they sailed for home.

It would be more than four years before the Inverness War Memorial was unveiled. An editorial in the *Inverness Courier* on Tuesday 19 December 1922 laid bare the painful emotions which the occasion evoked:

'We question if Inverness has ever witnessed a more impressive or a more inspiring sight that that which it saw on Saturday, when the Monument which has been erected to the memory of the 715 men belonging to the Burgh and Parish of Inverness who laid down their lives in the Great War was unveiled with simple and befitting ceremony. The vast gathering which assembled to do honour to the glorious dead was not only great in numbers and representative of every class in the community, but was charged with a common emotion and a common pride and alike by the reverence of its demeanour and the intentness with which it followed the proceedings testified to the greatness of the place which our fallen sons and brothers hold in the hearts of those for whom they gave their lives. For us of the present generation no visible monument of any kind is necessary to remind us of the suffering and the sorrow, the devotion and the sacrifice, the tragedies and the triumphs of the war. The names of those who suffered, of those who fought, of those who died, are enshrined in the hearts of those they loved. But already a generation is springing up to whom the war and all that it meant to those who lived through it, is but as a tale that is told, and as the years pass so will that generation grow in numbers, and the poignant living memories of the war become ever fewer and fewer. And that is why we of the present generation do well to erect our War memorials – symbols of sacrifice, symbols of suffering, symbols of gratitude for a great deliverance, above all symbols of the irreparable debt we owe, of the never-dying love we give to those who laid down their lives for us. To those who come after us these War Memorials will convey a message – a message of pride, perhaps, a message of faith, hope, and love assuredly, a message, let us pray, of warning and inspiration – of warning that war can only be waged at a great price in human life and human grief, of inspiration to count no sacrifice too great in the cause of humanity.

The monument which was unveiled on Saturday is in every respect a noble and worthy memorial to the men and the sacrifice it is intended to commemorate. In the sheer beauty and artistry of its conception and design, and in the skill and finish of its execution, it is altogether admirable, a veritable sermon in stone to all who look upon it. We are sure that not one of the thousands who saw it unveiled on Saturday, or who visited it subsequently, will grudge a word of congratulation to those responsible for it, the War memorial Committee who initiated and carried through the scheme, the architect who designed the monument, and the sculptors who executed it. They have given us a very beautiful and a very appropriate Memorial, one which no one who mourns a fallen father, husband, son, or brother can look upon without a feeling of reverence and hope, one which will convey to generations yet unborn an eloquent idea of the spirit in which the men of this generation responded to the call of duty, and fought and triumphed, and died in a high and holy cause.'

These words seem rather cloying and even slightly condescending to a modern audience, without a hint of self-doubt or anger at the waste of human life involved in the whole enterprise. But these were different times – when unquestioning loyalty to one's country and acceptance of the government's actions were almost universal – at least in public.

In the event, the monument, 33 feet high and in the form of a Celtic cross, was unveiled before a crowd of about 5000 people, including the relatives of 'the fallen'. The memorial was covered by an enormous Union Jack and was unveiled by The Mackintosh, as Lord Lieutenant of Inverness-shire and saluted by a detachment of Cameron Highlanders with their rifles reversed in honour of their dead comrades. It was designed by Mr J. Hinton Gall, architect and executed by

Messrs D. & A. Davidson, sculptors of Academy Street, Inverness, according to the *Courier*, in which coverage included almost verbatim accounts of the long speeches by Sir Donald Macdonald as Chairman of the War Memorial Committee, The Mackintosh and Provost Petrie.

Cavell Gardens was not the first choice of location. Initially the Committee had preferred a riverside site at the end of Ardross Street – once also considered for Flora Macdonald's statue. Cavell Gardens in the end seemed more appropriate, named as it was after Nurse Edith Cavell, shot by the Germans in Brussels in August 1915 for assisting French and British soldiers to cross the Dutch frontier – a capital offence under German military law, though her execution was seen as judicial murder in her native land.

World War One memorial at St Columba's parish church, with World War Two additions.

By this time Edwardian Inverness must have seemed a remote fantasy, a world which existed in the memory but which was lost and gone forever. In the years leading up to the outbreak of war in 1914, Highland society was unequal, hierarchical but stable. Landowners wielded tremendous power and estates operated in rigidly fixed ways where everybody knew their place. In Inverness, there were some rumblings of union power and female suffrage, but the working-class population of the town worked hard and, for the most part, accepted their fate. Emigration to the United States, Canada, Australia and New Zealand was still an attractive option.

In the aftermath of war a section of society attempted to keep the old traditions going, but their efforts seemed increasingly self-indulgent and anachronistic, though remarkably persistent.

INTO THE
MODERN AGE

DURING the inter-war period, Inverness did not exactly thrive. The history books say that the 1930s was a decade of depression, but for Inverness and many other small Scottish towns, the 1920s were not much better. As harsh as it might today sound, World War Two, when it came in the autumn of 1939, proved an economic godsend for Inverness.

Amongst the initial industrial casualties, in the early 1920s, were the breweries and distilleries in the town. Mergers and amalgamations meant

The British Cabinet met in the Town House on 7 September 1921. Lloyd George was on holiday at Gairloch when an Irish crisis arose. One of those present was Winston Churchill. ©Highland Photographic Archive

inevitable closures of small distilleries, though in Inverness the Glen Mhor and Glen Albyn distilleries, owned by Mackinlay and Birnie Ltd and Millburn distillery, owned by Grigors of Inverness, struggled on until the 1960s and 1970s. World War One, with its social dislocation of men and women and its substantial death toll, meant that post-war society would not be easy for anybody. In the upper echelons of society it was not so easy to attract servants – who had kept things running smoothly on the domestic front. The middle-classes, always rather reticent in Inverness, found that staffing for domestic service was becoming a big problem. The social changes were nationwide, so the previously insatiable demand for Highland girls to go into 'service' in Glasgow, Edinburgh and London no longer existed, leading to increased unemployment in rural areas and in the town of Inverness itself. This industry declined steadily throughout the 1920s and 1930s, only to nosedive to oblivion in the 1940s and 1950s. Then, 'Before the War' became the mantra of the middle-classes, looking back to an age of deference and solidity. Though, now at least, middle-class housewives could find solace in the new vacuum cleaners and washing machines which could mitigate the lack of willing servant girls.

Inverness escaped the worst of the economic depredations which turned much of industrial Britain into an economic wasteland, but there was genuine suffering in the Highland capital in the 1930s. There were soup kitchens and long queues at the 'Broo' – the Bureau of Labour, or the 'Labour Exchange', at which unemployed men and women registered for work. In the days before 'National Assistance' there were still Poorhouses in Inverness – cold, cheerless places with stone floors and few amenities and minimal furnishings. Charities rallied to the cause and the town authorities did what they could to alleviate distress. It was this painful experience which brought home to the Town Council that a more systematic approach to local government administration was required. There was

View from Tomnahurich hill.
©Highland Photographic Archive

*Inverness Castle. ©Highland
Photographic Archive*

obvious overcrowding in the older parts of the town, so plans were put in hand to build new houses for the labouring classes, in South Kessock (The Ferry) and Dalneigh. A start was made, but of course everything had to be put on hold once war broke out, once more, in 1939.

Before the growth of unemployment in the 1930s, obviously linked to wider economic forces, the authorities very much took the view that any able-bodied person who was fit for work should be employed and there was very little sympathy if the situation was otherwise. Indeed, until 1921 it was not possible to provide economic relief or support to able-bodied persons. Further improvements in this area had to await the great reforming social legislation of the post-war Labour Government of Clement Atlee.

The inter-war period was a time when the basic infrastructure needed for economic development in Inverness was put in place. Electricity and water supplies; a basic, though soon inadequate, sewerage system; increased public services; and a start on improving traffic management and transport infrastructure – all these projects made substantial progress in the 1930s. Planning was, however, haphazard, rather than integrated, storing up many problems for the future, when the basic systems needed, inevitably, to be replaced, often in their entirety.

One example of progress interrupted by the war was the project to build a new bridge across the Ness. A start was made and a temporary structure put in place which was to carry traffic until the new, wider bridge was built. It would replace the Suspension Bridge so familiar from old photographs of Inverness,

Friar's Street, 1920s.
©Highland
Photographic Archive

dating back to 1855. Adequate in the era of the horse and cart, it was hopelessly insufficient for the motorised age. More than anything else, wartime traffic underlined the need for a new bridge, but the war impoverished the nation and it was 1959 before anything happened. In that year the Suspension Bridge was closed and a temporary structure was used until the new concrete span opened on 28 September 1961.

The economic gloom of the Depression years was illuminated briefly in 1933, when Nessie was spotted in Loch Ness and launched on her modern career as a tourist attraction. For a few weeks in the spring of that year the *Inverness Courier*, which first broke the story and then all the national newspapers, descended on Inverness, determined to entertain and amuse their readers – and, of course, sell more newspapers. The situation rapidly descended into farce, but it was good fun while it lasted. It was good publicity for the area and perhaps even caused one or two more far-thinking locals to ponder the prospects of tourism as a viable industry for the Highlands.

It was also during the inter-war period that the foundations of Inverness as a centre of public administration were firmly laid. Local government was becoming more and more complex, with an appropriate structure of local government departments necessary to administer expanding public services. From housing to swimming pools, the Town Council in the Town House was bursting at the seams in its attempts to keep control of increasingly demanding services while making much needed plans for future improvements. Satellite offices sprang up around the town, though this fragmentation, if anything, made it more difficult to integrate services. Meanwhile, Inverness County Council was well established in the County Buildings on Glenurquhart Road.

In other areas of public service, health services were trying desperately to

29-31 High Street, Inverness.
©Highland Photographic Archive

Boots Library, High Street, in the 1930s. ©Highland Photographic Archive

respond to the increased demands of expanding population and social deprivation, while in education both the County and Inverness education authorities were developing centres of public administration. Indeed, from 1929 the educational administration of both the county and the burgh was transferred to the Education Committee of the County Council of Inverness. In the field of higher education, the reconstituted Inverness College, dating from 1920, brought demands for further skills. All these public services needed an increasingly skilled workforce – from secretarial levels upwards new technology, in the form of newfangled typewriters, calculating machines, reproduction machines, telephone systems and information retrieval and filing systems were stretching the army of public servants who were by far the largest workforce in the Highland capital.

It took an eternity for the administration of public services to catch up with the shambolic and sometimes corrupt reality. Not until the 1960s did national politicians summon up the collective courage to instigate local government reform and then only after a series of royal commissions and public investigations made some form of action almost inevitable. In the event, many felt the local

Inverness bus, 1930s, belonging to the Highland Transport Company; this company was founded in 1930, taking over Inverness and District Motor Services Ltd (1925). Nationalised 1952 as Highland Omnibuses, with headquarters in Bank Lane. ©Highland Photographic Archive

government reorganisations of the 1970s were too much of a compromise, clinging to outmoded geographical and social boundaries and the whole exercise had to be repeated in the 1990s. The current workforce would be naïve in thinking that it will not happen again during their professional careers.

The North of Scotland Milk Marketing Board, with its headquarters in Greig Street, came into existence in 1934. Alongside its offices were workshops and a creamery, opened in 1936. Covering the counties of Caithness, Sutherland, Ross &

Inverness Railway Station, 1930s. ©Highland Photographic Archive

Cromarty, Inverness and Nairn, with Moray added in 1944 and Orkney in 1946, this marketing enterprise perhaps gave notice of what could be achieved in economic development in the Highlands and Islands if an imaginative approach was adopted, backed by adequate funds and a skilled administration. In this respect it can be seen as a precursor of the economic development initiatives which eventually evolved into the Highlands and Islands Development Board (HIDB) of the 1960s and today's Highlands and Islands Enterprise (HIE) with its network of Local Enterprise Companies (LECs). By the 1990s the dairy industry had collapsed and the Inverness operation of the Milk Marketing Board was closed and demolished, to be replaced by modern housing.

An indication of the democratisation of society after World War One can be seen in the evolution of library services in Inverness. Following the adoption of the Public Libraries (Scotland) Acts of 1850 and 1867 a public library had been opened in Inverness on 12 June 1883, with Charles Fraser Mackintosh doing the honours, after years of campaigning. A library building was erected in Castle Wynd, with a School of Art on the upper floors. There were reading rooms for the public, with newspapers and magazines provided, but no direct access to the books, which had to be ordered up from library staff from a printed catalogue. An 'indicator board' advised the public whether the book they were interested in was on the premises or not. Not until 1932 was an 'open access' system introduced, allowing the public to browse among the books and select books for borrowing. At the same time the membership age limit of 14 was abolished and

*Leachkin Post Office, 1929.
In the* Daily Mail *Viscount
Rothermere is writing about
the need for a new political
party. He and Lord
Beaverbrook founded the
United Empire Party in 1929.
©Highland Photographic
Archive*

*Caledonian Hotel, 1930s.
Built 1780, enlarged 1822
and 1882, demolished 1966.
©Highland Photographic
Archive*

a juvenile membership category was introduced to include children of school age. At the time, these seemed revolutionary innovations.

Subsequently the library moved into one of the 1960s concrete boxes on Bridge Street, now occupied by Inverness Museum and then on to Farraline Park in 1981, to the classical frontage of Dr Bell's Institution, once a school, by then a Labour Exchange, Police Station, local government office and theatre. The building is completely unsuitable for delivering a modern public library service and indeed, according to local government standards for public libraries, provides only 50 per cent of the floor space needed for a library serving the population of Inverness. Plans have been dusted off at regular intervals, when public demand surfaces, for the provision of a state-of-the-art, integrated complex housing a modern public library, local government records and archives, local history collections and a genealogy service, with all the associated infrastructure of equipment, meeting rooms and adequate staffing. One measure of the local commitment to a celebratory Highland Year of Culture in 2007 will be whether these plans have come to fruition. They would represent a public commitment to the history and heritage of Inverness and the Highlands which has been sadly lacking up until now.

The Inverness Corporation Swimming Baths opened in 1936, showing that the Town Council could be just as committed to a healthy body as to a healthy mind. This was a vast improvement over the small privately owned swimming pool on Montague Row. Remodelled in 1983, the new baths were subsequently replaced by the Aquadome in the Bught Park in the 1990s, alongside a new running track and sports complex, which for all its financial problems represents a major commitment to the leisure infrastructure of Inverness.

*Empire Theatre,
Academy Street, in
the 1930s. The
theatre closed in
1970. ©Highland
Photographic Archive*

EMPIRE THEATRE

INVERNESS IN WORLD WAR TWO

DURING World War Two the Highlands north and west of the Great Glen became a Protected Area, a military zone within which all manner of activities took place, some of them highly secret. Commando training, convoy assembly, radio transmission and receiving stations, weapons ranges, naval and air bases – there was a lot going on and most of it involved passing through Inverness at one time or another. Even in and around the town, thousands of troops were stationed, running offices and performing a multitude of administrative functions, or undergoing training at the Cameron Barracks or Fort George. On the civilian front, there were some top-secret industrial activities taking place, notably the manufacture of the PLUTO 'pipeline under the ocean' which was an essential component of the planning for the invasion of Europe, providing essential fuel for the transport required on the other side. The war may have impoverished Britain, but it opened up Inverness and the Highlands to the possibilities of development. It may seem indelicate to say so, but as a marketing exercise, introducing thousands and thousands of service personnel, from both Britain and overseas, to the Highlands, it was an unparalleled success. It showed the necessity of adequate infrastructure without which a modern society would inevitably remain a backwater. Both the local population of the Highlands and the people running its institutions, could see the faint but decidedly rosy glow of prosperity and economic growth, though in ways which only the most far-seeing prophets could have predicted. In the meantime, the war itself would bring sadness and fear once more to the people of Inverness.

The public, having only 21 years earlier experienced a devastating world war, were all too well aware of the severity of the situation that now faced them, as evidenced in this editorial from the *Northern Chronicle* of 6 September 1939:

> 'It would be saying too much to pretend that it is possible at this moment to see the tragic events which have come upon us in the same perspective as the impartial historian. It is, nevertheless, true that the present conflict has been preceded by a longer period of reflection and what is at stake has been thrown into perspective more than has ever happened in any great war before...

INVERNESS BURGH AND COUNTY
WAR SAVING EFFORTS

DISTRICT	WAR WEAPONS WEEK. July, 1941.	WARSHIP WEEK. May, 1942.	TANKS FOR ATTACK. Aug.-Oct., 1942.	WINGS FOR VICTORY WEEK. June, 1943.	REPLACEMENT OF H.M.S. "SARACEN." Oct.-Dec., 1943.	SALUTE THE SOLDIER WEEK. June, 1944.	THANKSGIVING WEEK. October, 1945.	TOTALS.	PER HEAD OF POPULATION.		
Aird District . .	£71,184	£44,673	£15,759	£45,687	£37,849	£44,695	£28,461	£288,308	£35	18	1
Inverness District .	60,709	24,872	7,671	50,067	49,437	43,196	27,831	263,783	31	10	7
Badenoch . .	106,495	77,216	24,020	68,504	47,303	87,550	41,863	452,951	74	19	10
Kingussie Burgh .	31,955	11,665	7,415	28,897	18,813	30,791	14,390	143,926	110	14	3
Lochaber . .	68,855	60,521	19,471	67,586	37,086	71,026	52,118	376,663	46	1	0
Fort William Burgh	47,289	28,747	10,262	23,884	31,065	39,611	18,633	199,491	68	11	1
Skye . . .	117,634	63,059	18,166	65,270	51,079	64,644	47,869	427,721	52	10	9
Barra . .	12,805	3,248	1,824	10,864	6,712	4,767	4,254	44,474	29	13	0
North Uist .	15,066	5,684	3,405	6,721	7,978	9,017	7,814	55,685	23	14	0
South Uist .	20,801	5,935	3,078	32,464	22,169	8,944	19,385	112,776	24	1	1
Harris . . .	37,937	26,968	13,065	34,095	25,703	31,705	18,893	188,366	61	7	1
Total County .	£590,730	£352,588	£124,136	£434,039	£335,194	£435,946	£281,511	£2,554,144	£47	5	11
Burgh of Inverness .	356,558	215,693	116,918	213,357	219,177	265,555	195,310	1,582,568	68	16	2
Grand Totals .	£947,288	£568,281	£241,054	£647,396	£554,371	£701,501	£476,821	£4,136,712	£53	14	4
Of which Small Savings .	45·21 %	37·05 %	100 %	49·06 %	56·00 %	44·37 %	39·45 %	48.40 %	£26	0	1
Targets aimed at .	£300,000	£400,000	£200,000	£400,000	£350·000	£400,000	£400,000	£2,450,000	£30	0	0

The above is in addition to the normal Weekly Savings of the Population

Statistics of money raised in various war appeals, 1941-45 (from the collections of the Highland Folk Museum, Kingussie).

We are not merely fighting for Poland. We are in the strictest sense fighting for ourselves... nobody can imagine that a Germany drunk with power would have failed to attack sooner or later the free nations of the West. Events have shown that Hitlerism is old Prussianism writ large. If the idiom is to some extent new, the challenge to the world is one that has been heard before. It was successfully met a quarter of a century ago. It is an unspeakable tragedy that we should have to meet it again, but there can be no dubiety about the answer and this time it must be a final one.'

From the outbreak of war there was a great flurry of administrative activity. In 1939 it was announced that all able-bodied men between the ages of 18 and 40 would be eligible for military service. By the end of 1941 the upper limit was raised to 51 and, for the first time, single women between the ages of 20 and 30 were required to sign up for war work. Some registered for exemptions, either because of their 'reserved occupations' in industries deemed essential to the smooth and safe running of the country and of the war effort or, as some did on religious grounds, as 'conscientious objectors'.

Immediately the Defence of the Realm Regulations, preparations for which had been in place for some months, came into effect. Among these were laws regulating the black-out, not only of street lights but also of domestic and business premises, with wardens appointed to ensure compliance. Whilst the black-out was undoubtedly inconvenient, it also proved exciting for some – and it is also interesting to note how many women report that they never felt unsafe in Inverness in wartime conditions, despite the pitch-black streets. Black-out times were published in advance each week in local newspapers. There were, of course, accidents throughout Britain, many of which led to fatalities, caused by the dark conditions – for example drowning in the Caledonian Canal. With these dangers in mind, the time of a full moon was the most popular time for public entertainments and community events.

Plans for public air raid shelters were put into effect at Farraline Park, Castle Street, Bank Street and Merkinch and domestic Anderson Shelters were installed in back gardens. Every man, woman and child in the country was issued with an Identity Card and each was required to carry a gas mask. Babies were issued an all-in-one respirator that resembled a helmet with a bag attached. Evacuated children from the Edinburgh area arrived in Inverness aboard special trains. The evacuees placed great strain on local schools, where staff levels were already likely to be affected by the increasing enlistment of local men. A system of rationing for food, clothing, coal and petrol and many other items, both luxury and every-day was also instigated.

Though wartime restrictions would mean that the luxuries that made celebrations special were in short supply, there were plenty of opportunities for Invernessians to enjoy themselves. To maintain morale, it was thought expedient to allow sporting events to continue, so football matches and the fixtures of the North of Scotland Cricket Association were allowed to continue. As well as attending films and the theatre there were other entertainments and there was certainly no time to get bored for the wartime civilian – there was plenty of war work, both official and unofficial to do. Socks had to be knitted for the forces, spaghnum moss gathered (for use in field dressings) and numerous government campaigns were established for all manner of fund-raising such as buying war-time bonds and national savings certificates. Scrap metal, old pots and pans and even railings were collected for melting-down to use in the building of war planes, although recently-discovered evidence suggests that the metal collected was quite unsuitable for aeroplane manufacture and the project was introduced as much to raise the morale of civilians who felt glad to be able to help in some way.

Inverness was used to its role as a quiet market town, but for six years, during the war and within the lifetime of many of its residents, it became an important and cosmopolitan hub of military activity. The role of the military in society had a far higher profile than we are used to in these times of defence cuts and regimental amalgamations. The Cameron Barracks, overlooking Millburn Road, were an important regimental depot and training establishment, while Fort George, a few miles out of town at Ardersier, was of equal status. Many thousands of soldiers in the British Army passed through Inverness in the course of their careers and during wartime there was an intense concentration of military activity in and around the town. For some, duties were relatively routine, bordering on the boring, for those who worked in office jobs, maintenance depots and on guard duties. For others, a visit to Inverness was a welcome break from intense commando training, or practising for the D-Day landings. For naval and air crew, there were periods of intense action, followed by relative inactivity and relaxation.

The whole of the Moray Firth area from Tain and Dornoch to Ardersier, Nairn, Elgin and Lossiemouth was an area of intense military activity, with naval bases, shore stations, air fields, training establishments, maintenance depots and barracks. Combined Operations Staff took over the Cameron Barracks later in the war and used the beaches of Easter Ross and the Black Isle to rehearse the D-Day landings. An Army Command covering the whole of the north of Scotland from Aberdeen to the Northern Isles and the Hebrides and a Fighter Command HQ for the whole of Scotland were established in Inverness. The Longman airfield was greatly expanded and was used by many distinguished visitors, including the King, on his way to visit Scapa Flow in October 1939. Dalcross airfield was established as a training base where thousands of air gunners were trained. The Admiralty established a programme of coastal patrols and mine-watching patrols in the Moray Firth. Further afield in the Highlands, there were naval bases and radio stations on the west coast and the islands concerned with Atlantic patrols and convoy duties, while in the central Highlands, especially around Aviemore and near Fort William (Achnacarry), there was intense commando training for both British and foreign troops. Later in the war there were prisoner of war camps, in the Cairngorms, in the Black Isle and Easter Ross and elsewhere.

Inverness was also the centre of government civilian administration for the north of Scotland, with local HQs for the Civil Defence authorities, the Ministry of Food, the Ministry of Fuel and other wartime departments. There were also many foreign civilians in the area, notably members of the Canadian Forestry Corps and the Newfoundland Forestry Units who worked in the Cairngorms and elsewhere and were frequent visitors to Inverness. Service personnel from the Dominions and the US also visited Inverness in large numbers, sometimes on leave, looking for relatives and ancestral homes. Towards the end of the war the Queensgate Hotel in Inverness was used as a hospitality centre for these foreign soldiers. There were Polish troops in the area and many Norwegians training for commando warfare.

The sensitive nature of many of the military operations meant that there was a noticeable impact on the civilian population. Movement within the Protected Area north and west of the Great Glen was severely restricted from February 1940. To enter the area a permit was required and residents had to have a Certificate of Residence, issued by local police. Further security was ensured by the establishment in Inverness of a Government Censorship Department. All letters posted for delivery outwith the area were checked and if necessary censored and telephone conversations and telegrams were also monitored. These measures were more restrictive than in most other parts of the UK.

Local newspapers were published in severely shortened versions to save on newsprint and were subject to censorship and publication rules. For once, it is impossible to rely on them for local history, except in a distorted and incomplete version. Reading between the lines an enemy agent might conclude from the

Supporters of the Comfort Fund in the Caledonian Hotel, Inverness, showing the woollen clothing and blankets they have collected. ©Highland Photographic Archive

number of entertainments listed that the inhabitants of Inverness had not in fact embarked on an era of sybaritic self-gratification and amusement, or responded to a tourist boom, but were playing host to thousands of non-civilian visitors. Most local hotels and the Northern Meeting Rooms with their capacious ballroom, were requisitioned for the use of service personnel, but alternative venues were found. The war was however a disaster for tourism and for example the sailings of the Gondolier between Inverness and Fort William were suspended in 1939.

Invernessians who remember the war years – most of whom would have been quite young at the time – look back on that period with a mixture of sadness and nostalgia. Though, of course, the war was not treated lightly, it had its own peculiar excitement, especially for children. Especially too, perhaps, for young, single women, who could have their pick of handsome young soldiers, sailors and airmen. Inevitably romance blossomed in wartime Inverness and after the war Inverness war brides found themselves distributed around the UK and across the world.

If the local press was uncharacteristically silent about the presence of military personnel in the area, with all the associated social problems, they were relied upon by Invernessians for their coverage of the wider war, both nationally and internationally. Although the news they provided was not often current and always highly-censored, there is a surprising amount of coverage of foreign campaigns. As the 51st Highland Division was arguably the single best-known fighting unit in the British Army, with Highlanders well represented in many other regiments, this is perhaps not all that unexpected. Letters from overseas personnel and from POW camps in Europe, were also published – most of the original Highland Division was captured at St Valery in the Dunkirk fiasco.

A sadder aspect of coverage of the war in local newspapers was, of course, the reporting of deaths and casualties. Typically, a photograph of the dead soldier was used in the local press, especially in the *Highland News*. His local connections would be detailed and there was a special section in the Death Notices for military casualties. Officers, or men with some standing in the local community, would attract a more lengthy write-up. Especially after the great losses at Dunkirk, but also after El Alamein and other engagements, locals would scour the casualty lists for loved ones in the lists of killed, wounded, captured or missing in action.

One feature of wartime newspapers which is of great interest to modern readers are the many patriotic adverts for cigarettes and other goods which managed always to incorporate a war message into the sales pitch. Thus, British Railways were 'The Vital Link – Carrying the War Load' and passengers were asked to be patient and to expect delays. In 1944 the people were enjoined: 'Do not invade the trains THIS EASTER' – the capacity was needed to transport 'men and materials for our Fighting Forces'. What they could not say was that this was part of the build-up for the D-Day landings which would take place in June.

On the industrial front, Holm Woollen Mills had a contract for army blankets, initially providing 1000 a week, dropping to 500 when labour shortages

2nd Battalion of the Queen's Own Cameron Highlanders disbanding at Cameron Barracks, 1948. ©Highland Photographic Archive

started to hit. The Rose Street Foundry is most famous for its part in the PLUTO project, but also produced all manner of other machinery and crucial parts.

The war in Europe ended on Tuesday 8 May 1945. The celebrations in Inverness were unrestrained and ecstatic, as throughout the whole country. Church bells rang and special services of thanksgiving were held. Mr Cameron, the Town Clerk, intimated in a Public Notice that a Reception and Dinner organised by the Town Council would be held. Butchers' shops in Inverness closed for two days and grocers' shops were to close at 1pm on VE Day and would be closed on Wednesday. It would take some days for some measure of normality to resume, as the entire population had some serious sobering up to do, whether from the effects of alcohol or from the euphoria of Victory.

Brooke Bond Dividend Tea (1s 7d a lb) put a triumphant advert on the front page of the *Inverness Courier*:

'Victory has come

The Huns are beaten, their military power ended.

For this and much more the Nation owes

an eternal debt of gratitude to all our fighting services.

With united hearts we salute them; they must never be forgotten

*   *   *

This brings the day of freedom from control

nearer, when, among other things, you will be

able to get as much as you like of "the brand of tea you prefer."

All due to the heroism and sacrifice of gallant men and patient women.'

The *Inverness Courier* editorialised in similar vein:

'Deliverance

We have reached one of the supreme moments in human history. Never, in fact, has there been a moment like it before and pray God there will never be a moment like it again. For it is not merely a military victory of a kind and of a magnitude without precedence in human history which we are celebrating to-day, but a mighty deliverance – a deliverance from the greatest assault which the powers of evil have ever launched against the mind, the body and the soul of man. Thus the arrogant, blood-thirsty, unscrupulous Power, which five-and-a-half years ago set out to conquer the world, has drunk to the dregs the cup of humiliation and defeat...

The dawn has broken upon us fair and glorious, but what of the day to which it is the herald? Never has there been a moment so pregnant with fate as this. Never has opportunity so great been put into the hands of mortal men. Civilisation has come to one of its cross-roads. It has come to cross-roads before, but it rarely perceived them, or if it did it saw them but dimly and uncomprehendingly. But to-day the cross-roads are glittering under the rays of the rising sun, plain for all men to see – if they will. As we choose our road now so will the future of the world for countless generations be.'

Immediately after the Prime Minister's broadcast at 3pm on Tuesday 10 May, services of thanksgiving were held in all the local churches and were attended by very large congregations. Although men and women of the Services – on duty in Inverness – and the young people naturally expressed their joy at the cessation of hostilities in less restrained fashion than older townsfolk, the crowds which thronged the streets were, for the most part very well behaved and there was less boisterous celebration than might have been expected. This was largely due to the fact that much of the country had known the end was imminent for several days and the delay in official notification of the cease fire had robbed the occasion of much of the spontaneity it would have otherwise possessed. After the anticipation of the previous few days there was something of an anti-climax and it was not long before the realisation that the war with Japan had still to be won tended towards a more sober celebration. At the same time the general feeling of relief and thankfulness that the European was over was very evident.

The celebrations of the next day were memorable. There were three services of thanksgiving in the Cathedral, at 11 am, 6pm and 8pm and when the cathedral's Provost found the church half full of people in mid-afternoon he laid on an extra, informal service. At night there was a Victory Ball in the Caledonian Hotel Ballroom attended by over 500 people. They raised £308 15s for the Inverness Burgh Welcome Home Fund.

The weather was rainy in the morning and kept many revellers indoors, but in the afternoon the sun came out and the open-air celebrations planned for the Castle hill went ahead with a religious service and a concert by the military band of the Queen's Own Cameron Highlanders. It was a matter of great regret that no pipe band could be summoned – the pipers were all on leave! The *Inverness Courier* captured the mood of the day:

'VICTORY DAY HOLIDAYS
Inverness and North Celebrations
RELIGIOUS SERVICES
BONFIRES AND DANCES'

Great crowds thronged the streets of Inverness on the Victory Day holidays. Public buildings and private houses flew the flags of the United Nations and bonfires were lit in the town and on the surrounding hills.' Of course, the UN was not founded until later that year.

As with most public celebrations, a few revellers allowed themselves to be carried away in all the excitement. Newspapers reported a few instances of hooliganism and that some flags were stolen from buildings, but even these instances were mostly good-humoured.

On Sunday 13 May there was an official Victory Parade and more thanks-giving services. Intimations of apparent normality could be seen in the newspaper reports, where accounts of the parade were flanked by a report that on the previous Friday Lieutenant-Colonel W. H. Lane of Glenmoriston had seen the Loch Ness Monster through 'strong field glasses' in perfect viewing conditions. Of course, the events of May were just a taster for the celebrations to come in August. Following the initial shock of the use of the atomic bomb, there was scarcely-concealed joy when the Japanese surrender was announced by the Prime Minister in a broadcast at midnight on Tuesday 14 August. The war was over. The *Inverness Courier* gave a rollicking account of subsequent festivities:

'VICTORY CELEBRATIONS IN THE HIGHLANDS

Peace Proclaimed With Bonfires and Rejoicing

Victory was celebrated joyously throughout the Highlands. In every town and village bonfires were lit and flags of the United Nations were flown from houses and public buildings.

Immediately after the news of victory was broadcast at midnight on Tuesday, church bells were rung in many of the country districts and big bonfires were lit on the hills … Fireworks were set off and large crowds congregated in the centre of the town. Bonfires were lit in the main streets and one policeman, who endeavoured to restrain some of the less responsible onlookers, was hoisted shoulder-high. Owing to the fire danger squads of NFS men were on duty.

Inverness Castle was flood-lit last night, and the effect was both striking and beautiful. Verey lights were fired from the Castle after dark, and the river was lit up by the flames, some of which burned on after striking the water.

Great crowds thronged the streets of the town on Wednesday and a huge bonfire was lit in the middle of High Street. Tea chests, empty beer barrels and even hurleys, which had been left unattended, were piled on the fire and motorists had difficulty making progress. At night there were bonfires in every part of the town and, as palings and garden gates were torn up and used as firewood, a good deal of destruction was caused. Shortly before midnight a pipe band appeared and marched along High Street followed by great crowds of Servicemen and women and civilians linked arm in arm. The band afterwards played selections at the Exchange and reels were danced.'

The shockingly gaunt, almost-skeletal prisoners of war returning from the Far East provided timely reminders, as if any were needed, of the suffering those armed forces had endured. Meanwhile, many of the soldiers and POWs returning from Europe had witnessed scenes to horrific they could hardly bear to talk about it. Once the euphoria of victory had worn off, there were immense social problems to be confronted but with an impoverished national exchequer. The particular problems of the Highlands were high on a scale of national priorities facing the Labour Secretary of State for Scotland, Tom Johnston. His visionary views on the Highland economy would have far-reaching effects over the next 50 years.

ON THE ROAD TO A NEW MILLENNIUM

IN the aftermath of World War Two, the priority for the burgh authorities in Inverness was housing. The need was great, with severe overcrowding in the tenements of Eastgate and Castle Street and a tremendous demand for new houses by returning servicemen. However, it was to be many years before the Town Council could be in a position to take decisive action and not until the mid-1950s did plans for new housing start to be implemented at anything approaching an appropriate scale, though a good start was made in 1948 and 1949.

As ever, the problem was financing – the Depression of the 1930s followed by World War Two had left a serious deficit in both funding and housing. Plans for the building of new 'social' housing – what we would call council houses – in Merkinch, Hilton and

Inverness High School.

Dalneigh were put forward and the best answer to provide decent housing at affordable rents seemed to be to import from Sweden what were effectively house kits. After the Burgh Treasurer did his sums the proposed rents seemed impossibly high and were reduced. This may have made social housing more affordable for the average family, but it made it completely unaffordable for the Burgh and much of the newspaper coverage of this issue throughout the 1950s and 1960s concerns the council lurching from one financial crisis to the next.

Unsurprisingly, financial crisis was a national as well as a local malaise and somehow everybody muddled through. Ultimately, as the economy improved steadily through the 1960s, householders got used to paying more. They could now afford some of the basic luxuries of modern society: television, once impossibly expensive, became commonplace and ownership of a motor car was within the capability of the average family. We too easily forget that many of the things we now take for granted were, before 1960 – like washing machines, fitted carpets and telephones – well beyond the means of most citizens.

The spring of 1945 had seen Winston Churchill thrown out of office by an

The Palace Hotel, with Craig Phadrig and Scorguie behind.

electorate grateful for his war leadership but now deeply suspicious of his social policy. They elected a Labour government by a landslide, backed by the votes of servicemen and women, many of them still overseas. The immediate post-war period was one of political optimism and sweeping reforms: the Education Act of 1944, the creation of the National Health Service, the nationalisation of coal, rail and transport industries.

In this context, it seemed outrageous that men (and, to a lesser extent, women) who had served their country in its hour of need could be treated so shabbily when they got home and became civilians again. There were many reasons for this, among them the sheer scale of the problem and the financial insolvency of the nation. Neither were politicians used to dealing with raised expectations on this scale and the civil service infrastructure was not prepared to implement such radical reform and could not cope with the scale of administrative input required.

Some might argue that it was not really until the radical administration of Margaret Thatcher in the 1980s that the country submitted to the 'reality check' required and the general unpopularity of Thatcherite policies throughout Scotland in the 1980s played an important role in popularising calls for self-government – nationalists wanted independence, others preferred devolution. The first manifestation of post-war outrage in Inverness, however, had come as early

The scar of 1960s architecture in Bridge Street.

as the summer of 1946 when squatters occupied former War Department huts and buildings. About 41 families in Inverness occupied sites at the Longman Aerodrome, Raigmore Wood, Annfield Road, Porterfield Road and Muirtown. Sanitary con-

Co-op at 59-65 Church Street in the 1950s (Scottish Midland Cooperative Society). ©*Highland Photographic Archive*

ditions were poor. All were ex-servicemen, with their wives and young children. The largest squatter colony in Inverness was at the Longman site, where 20 families moved into huts recently vacated by the Air Ministry. Similar demonstrations were occurring all over the country, as a protest against the seeming callous disregard by the authorities of the need for housing.

At Raigmore, at the end of August 1946, six families moved into huts owned by the Air Ministry and which had been lying empty since November 1945. These families included ten children ranging in ages from 15 months to nine years. One of the families had been on the housing list, waiting for a house, for nine years. Not all of the empty huts were occupied at once and some wrote their names on notices which were pinned to the doors, staking a claim to future occupancy. One of the Porterfield huts was occupied by a family who had previously been living in a tent in the Haugh district because they could not get a house of their own from the Council.

The squatters attracted a lot of sympathy throughout the town and a lot of newspaper coverage. Many thought that the empty huts should already have been used as a temporary remedy for the housing shortage and, bowing to public opinion and practicalities, the Town Council offered the use of council employees to make some of the huts more habitable, by connecting lighting and improving sanitation arrangements. Many of the squatters let it be known that they were willing to pay rent and they hoped that they would be allowed to stay. They also hoped that, at a national level, the government would find some way to legalise and to regularise their position. This hope proved misplaced.

Two years later the squatters were still there. In December 1948, just before Christmas, the Secretary of State for Scotland was successful in getting eviction

Young & Chapman, 15-17 Union Street, 1940s. ©Highland Photographic Archive

orders against six of the Raigmore squatters. Meanwhile, the Town Council had begun addressing the problem of housing and had made a start on two new housing schemes, at Dalneigh and Hilton. The Dalneigh Housing Site was the first to be started and, over the next five years, was steadily extended.

A feature of the new housing estate was the new 'Swedish' houses, purchased directly from Swedish suppliers in prefabricated form and assembled in Inverness. At a sitting of the Inverness Dean of Guild Court (the planning authority) on 7

Melven Brothers' Bookshop at 29 Union Street, 1940s. ©Highland Photographic Archive

January 1946 permission was granted to the Scottish Special Housing Association to erect 64 permanent houses 'of the Swedish type' at Dalneigh and at a meeting of the Housing Committee of the Town Council on the same night it was agreed to erect 'aluminium houses' at sites on Harrowden Road, Coronation Park, Bruce Avenue, Ballifeary Road and Culduthel Road.

The public were sceptical. A correspondent calling himself 'Hope Deferred' wrote to the *Inverness Courier* in June 1946 to say that local housing policy seemed to be 'in a stupid and foolish muddle'.

The Council, he claimed, had started building 20 houses in Bruce Gardens in November 1944, but they would not be ready until November 1946 and perhaps not even then. In August 1946 the Inverness Trades and Labour Council protested to the Secretary of State in the strongest possible terms about the delay in providing housing.

The Burgh Surveyor, Mr I. W. Jack, reported in June 1946 that the total cost of housing schemes under construction was £657,250, which would provide 650 new houses. The work force required and its contribution to the local economy, was considerable. Again, this situation was replicated throughout the land. Today, the idea of building a new house for just over £1000 seems impossible, but it gives a graphic insight into how much the cost of living has increased – to people who remember those days, it is today's prices that seem surreal.

By January 1948 the Burgh Architect, Mr J. Blackburn, was able to report progress: 32 houses were rapidly approaching completion at Hilton when, at the end of 1946, no house-building at all had yet started and at Dalneigh, 64 Swedish houses were now finished. By mid-November 1948 Mr Blackburn was able to report the purchase of a further 100 Swedish houses, to be erected at Dalneigh, beginning in the spring of 1949.

However, in November 1949 the Town Council's Housing Committee had to address the difficult question of housing allocation for the Swedish houses. They worked out that the 'economic' rent for a Swedish house worked out at about £65 a year, though even this figure was considerably underestimated. As one Councillor pointed out, there was no point in allocating such a house to an ordinary working man earning £5 a week if he would have to pay £2 a week in rent and rates. The proposed solution was to move council tenants with a higher income into the newer houses and to allow those with a lower income to occupy existing housing. In due time, the names and addresses of the successful tenants for the new houses in the Hilton and Dalneigh schemes were published in the local press for all to see.

This aspect of local government – responsibility for housing – perhaps caused more aggravation for all concerned than any other council service. The deliberations of the Housing Committee were, inevitably, subject to abuse and stories are still told in the town of brown envelopes being handed to influential Councillors in an attempt to improve somebody's position on the housing waiting list. Sour grapes? Perhaps – an element of envy and disappointment is a

Coronation Park, 1950s. The school on the left closed in the 1970s. ©Highland Photographic Archive

dangerous mix. In retrospect, in view of what is now known about the workings of local government generally throughout Britain in the post-war period and in view of what we all know about human nature, it seems unlikely that there were no abuses.

As the 20th century reached its third quarter, one of the features of life in Inverness was the reform of local government – which happened not once, but twice. In 1975 the Burgh of Inverness ceased to exist and was replaced by a local government unit called Inverness District Council, encompassing not only the boundaries of the former burgh but also a portion of the mainland part of what had previously been the County of Inverness-shire. At the same time, a Highland Region was created, under the control of Highland Regional Council, containing eight District Council areas: Inverness, Nairn, Caithness, Sutherland, Lochaber, Skye & Lochalsh, Ross & Cromarty and Badenoch & Strathspey.

This reorganisation of local government had important implications throughout Scotland and certainly in Inverness. Local government administration became much tighter and working practices which were acceptable in the 1960s had to be changed. This was a difficult time for many local government officers who had dedicated their entire working lives to public service and now found their integrity called into question. Many took the chance for early retirement, or decided to try their luck in consultancy work or in another career. Some were disillusioned, but others just got on with the job and made the best of it, though not without considerable trepidation. At least there seemed to be an opportunity for investment in public services, with perhaps improvements long aspired to.

This atmosphere of upheaval thus brought changes in local government personnel. Burgh officials had often not been natives of Inverness, but now it seemed

Farraline Park, 1962.
©Highland Photographic
Archive

Melven Brothers' Bookshop,
29 Union Street, 1950s.
©Highland Photographic
Archive

that the whole operation was being run by 'incomers'. This was an exaggeration, but there were many people who used the 1975 reorganisation as an opportunity for a career move, or even a lifestyle change, preferring the quality of life and environment in the Highlands to the urban rat-race. Some of the new arrivals took a while to become used to the way things work in the Highlands, where an informal network has long paralleled the more formal mechanisms of governance. It was not an easy time and the whole process was repeated in April 1996 when yet another reorganisation of local government in Scotland came into effect.

Again there were far-reaching consequences for council employees and their

Gilbert Street, Merkinch, 1957. ©Highland Photographic Archive

families, who faced a major upheaval in their lives – in some cases for the second time in their careers. Both the Highland Regional Council and the eight District Councils created in 1975 were abolished and replaced by the Highland Council, a new 'unitary authority' combining the functions of its nine predecessors. Another clearout ensued, with many long-serving officers taking retirement as an option preferable to service under the new regime.

Change, it seems, is often brutal. With the emergence of the Scottish Executive as the administrative wing of the revived Scottish Parliament in 1999, it was inevitable that the committee structure of local government would come to mirror the reformed structure of Scottish government. This has meant the elimination of many existing local government departments and their amalgamation into a reduced number of 'Services'. Inevitably, this has limited the opportunities for people to become involved in local government as Councillors, although somehow the number of local government officials continues to proliferate as the

Gasworks, 1960. ©Highland Photographic Archive

new public services get into their stride and begin to address public expectations of what they should be doing.

Of course it is no bad thing that local government in all its aspects has become increasingly professionalised, if that means the elimination of the possibility of favouritism and corruption which often tainted it in the past. But it is difficult not to look back with nostalgia to the more easy-going times, especially before 1975, when complacency and mediocrity were not the crimes they are today.

New Fire Station, 1960.
©Highland Photographic
Archive

Inevitably, some find it difficult to let go of the past. 'Inverness' which, as a local government unit, now extends from Beauly to Ardersier and from Culloden to Fort Augustus, still maintains the illusion of Victorian civic government with a 'Provost of Inverness', complete with robes, chain of office and a funny hat. There is even a movement to reconstitute the Burgh of Inverness as a unit of government, leaving the rural hinterland adrift to fend for themselves in the local corridors of power. Then there was the campaign to have Inverness declared a 'city', which admittedly had more to do with pursuing inward investment than any genuine 'civic' pride, but which absorbed an excessive amount of collective local energy before 'city status' was finally achieved in 2000, as did the misplaced and unsuccessful bid for Inverness to become the European 'Capital of Culture' in 2008 – a campaign since replaced by a much more realistic celebration of a 'Year of Culture' in 2007. To some these backward-looking manifestations do not sit easily with the concept of 'modern' local government, 'fit for the 21st century', as the local spin-doctors would have it. But nor does a perception of council dissembling in its dealings with the public and the media sit well with 'open government'. Spin-doctors do not like bright lights and fresh air. And does change always have to be brutal, with management bullying and wrecked lives? The council's recognition of 'stress' as an issue which, in the end, affects service delivery adversely, is much to be welcomed.

Apart from the housing and population explosion of the last 50 years and the reform of local government which has made Inverness such an administrative

*R.S. MacDonald & Co
tailor's shop on corner of
Crown Road and Millburn
Road, demolished to make
way for the Eastgate Centre
(completed 1983). ©Highland
Photographic Archive*

powerhouse, an important aspect in which Highland life has changed dramatically, especially in the last years of the 20th century, concerns transport and traffic management.

In Inverness itself the circulation of traffic around the town centre, or if we are to be more contemporary, the city centre, is something which has changed local commercial life greatly. The pedestrianisation of High Street, albeit with street furniture and fittings perhaps more appropriate to an English market town than to an historic Scottish burgh, has improved the quality of retail therapy for the local population.

A multi-storey car park helped ease traffic congestion, at least for a while. In the 1980s came the Eastgate Centre, sweeping away historic tenements, shops and pubs for a new shopping mall – extended across the road into Eastgate II in 2003. A new bridge across the Ness, the Friar's Bridge, opened in 1987, taking traffic destined for Fort William and Beauly around the centre of town. Some worried about this new bridge fulfiling one of the Brahan Seer's prophecies that the Highlands would be overrun 'by ministers without grace and women without shame'. Then again...

The new concrete bridge over the Ness, started in 1939 and finally replacing the old Suspension Bridge in 1961, stylistically matched the concrete boxes of Bridge Street. Further afield, the Kessock Bridge opened in 1982, hurrying visitors over the water to the north as part of the improvement of the A9 from Perth to Inverness and northward across the Black Isle to Dingwall and Dornoch.

Meanwhile, the development of air travel which started in 1946 with the announcement of a new air service linking Aberdeen, Inverness and Stornoway expanded steadily until now there are direct links to two London airports: Gatwick and Luton.

Queuing for the sales at The Fashion Salon, 9-10 Union Street, in the 1950s. ©Highland Photographic Archive

All of these changes have improved the quality of life for the residents of Inverness, though native Invernessians, like contemporaries around the world, often look back nostalgically to the days of their youth. Certainly the population of Scotland and the rest of the British Isles – and further afield – have been voting with their feet over the years, turning Inverness into one of the fastest growing urban centres in the country. Since 1900 and especially since 1960, the local population has increased dramatically:

1901	21,238
1911	22,216
1921	20,944
1931	22,583
1951	28,107
1961	29,774

Thereafter, comparisons get a little tricky, as changes in the way the Census Office publishes its figures and changes in what is meant by 'Inverness' make direct comparisons difficult. By 1991 the population of the 'Inverness Settlement Zone' was 41,766, but this rises to 50,494 if the new housing estates to the east of the burgh around Smithton, Cradlehall, Culloden and Balloch are included. By 2001 this total had risen to 60,000 – a massive growth but still very small for a city.

Inverness Motor Company Ltd, Strothers Lane. ©Highland Photographic Archive

One of the most obvious observations about Inverness at the end of the 20th century is that while traditional local industries continued to decline in the post-war period, service industries and administration flourished. We have already looked at local government administration in some detail, but Inverness was also the home of the Highlands and Islands Development Board (now Highlands and Islands Enterprise), itself with a large workforce. Raigmore Hospital expanded and grew and, by the end of the century, was a major employer and important medical centre for both treatment and research. The Crofters' Commission

Walker's Emporium, corner of Inglis Street and Baron Taylor Street, 1950s. ©Highland Photographic Archive

occupied part of the concrete boxes on Bridge Street and many other, smaller agencies opened local or national offices in Inverness: An Comunn Gaidhealach, the Red Deer Commission, Scottish Natural Heritage, the Forestry Commission (now Forest Enterprise), as well as banks, building societies, voluntary organisations and charities. Inverness's role as a centre of administration and government partly explains the influx of population and the development of services and retail outlets to service the incomers. With the newcomers came the need for new schools, the expansion of Inverness College and the creation of the University of the Highlands and Islands. Sports and leisure facilities were created or improved, centred around the Bught area of the town. Eden Court Theatre provided a magnificent cultural facility. New industries moved into the Longman and Harbour Road became one long car showroom. Last, but certainly not of least importance in the cultural life of the city, the amalgamation of two of Inverness's historic football clubs, Inverness Caley and Inverness Thistle, created the (currently) successful Inverness Caledonian Thistle Football Club, with a new stadium on the Longman.

Inverness celebrated the new Millennium at the beginning of 2000 with some confidence in its future prospects and prosperity, if not a grasp of arithmetic – we have already seen how our Victorian ancestors correctly marked the start of the 20th century on 1 January 1901. It is now time to look at possibilities for the 21st century.

Bridge and castle in 1890s. The 'castle' was built in 1833-6. The buildings between the bridge and the castle are 'Castle Tolmie', demolished in the 1960s. ©Highland Photographic Archive

Execrable 1960s concrete boxes at the bottom of Bridge Street; the one on the left was occupied by the Highlands and Islands Development Board, renamed Highland and Islands Enterprise, until their removal to the Inverness Retail Park in 2002.

INTO THE 21ST CENTURY

T HE City of Inverness, in the early years of the 21st century, is still in the throes of expansion, without any signs of economic decline. New industries have sprung up, most notably Inverness Medical, at the centre of a medical technology complex alongside Raigmore Hospital and there is still room on the Longman Industrial Estate for more new businesses. A new business

Kessock Ferry, Eilean Dubh.
©*Highland Photographic Archive*

park has been developed at Beechwood and the new Inverness Retail and Business Park has mushroomed on the Golden Mile, along the A96 east of Inverness, with a supermarket, cinema complex, bookshop and other retail stores as well as the relocated headquarters of High-

Greig Street suspension bridge.

lands and Islands Enterprise. Further developments in this area are anticipated in the next decade, including improved road access to Inverness Airport at Dalcross.

The proliferation – and decline – of health and fitness clubs is one sure indication of economic, as well as physical, good health and this industry seems to be becoming an integral part of local life style and not just with the younger age group. Ruthless competition has meant some casualties along the way, but most of these glassy, glossy premises seem here to stay. At the other end of the leisure spectrum, eating out at a good restaurant and putting back all the pounds lost in the fitness clubs is no longer a rare experience in Inverness, with several

Station Square: the headquarters of the Highland Railway, the Station Hotel (now the Royal Highland Hotel) and the execrable entrance to the railway station.

excellent eateries to choose from alongside the usual fast-food and food-chain outlets.

On the cultural side, improvements at Inverness Museum and Art Gallery have produced an excellent introduction to Highland history and culture for visitors and locals alike. Eden Court Theatre promises renovation and expansion in the next few years. Inverness Library, a mainstay of local culture since 1883, is the repository of local history and culture for both Inverness and the Highlands, with excellent collections of books and periodicals. It is also now connected to the Internet, with free access for learning, research and leisure purposes, including an email facility, which makes it popular with tourists and other visitors.

Inverness Library, located at the back of the renovated bus station at Farraline Park, is located in what was once Dr Bell's school. The building, which is not really suited to modern library services, also houses the Highland Archives. The archivist and his staff, as well as preserving the records of the Burgh of Inverness and its successors, also offer a genealogy service to anybody wishing to trace their ancestors.

Union Street.

On the down side, it is obvious that Inverness does not now view high culture amongst its top priorities, which is perhaps why the Capital of Culture bid failed. Inverness was a town which preferred a new sports and leisure complex, a new swimming pool, a new running track, a new football stadium, three new shopping malls, a new supermarket and a crematorium to a much-needed cultural complex. Inverness Museum is bursting at the seams and leaking in its roof, Balnain House – 'the Home of Highland Music' – has closed, the one remaining independent cinema has closed, the archival heritage of the Highlands is dispersed in inadequate stores, its genealogical research service is only as efficient as its understaffing and under-resourcing allows and the floor space of Inverness Library is, as we have seen, half of what it should be for the population. There

Supermarket and traffic management, Rose Street; on the horizon is the distinctive profile of Craig Phadrig hill fort.

Inverness Museum, Bridge Street.

The pedestrianised High Street.

135

High Street and the Steeple rising above the original town prison.

have been numerous reports and consultancy studies over the last 20 years addressing some or all of these needs and currently all those interested in the arts, culture, history and heritage of the Highlands, including Inverness, are pinning their hopes on the prize of Year of Culture 2007. There is a real expectation that, finally, an integrated arts, local history, archives and genealogy centre, with appropriate technology, conference, exhibition and research facilities can be established in Inverness.

There is tremendous local enthusiasm for local history, culture and the arts. As discussed earlier, the work of the Inverness Local History Forum; the Inverness Field Club; the Gaelic Society of Inverness with its worldwide membership; the local history evening classes organised by the Workers' Educational Association and the University of Aberdeen's KEY Learning Opportunities; as well as the Highland Family History Society all serve the needs and interests of those fascinated by the history and traditions of the Highlands. Indeed, all over the Highlands local history groups, heritage centre and museums are sprouting up – over 100 at the latest count – along with their websites. With this reservoir of enthusiasm and expertise and with a massive North American market for family history, local history and Highland culture, it is perhaps surprising that no private entrepreneur has stepped in to fill the vacuum left by public authorities.

The population of Inverness will continue to grow over the next decade and if current trends are maintained the housing boom will continue for some years yet. We have seen the tide of housing creep up the slopes of Craig Phadrig over the last 20 years and there are still plenty of available gaps to be filled, especially to the east of Inverness. Many locals shake their heads at the number of new houses being built, year on year and wonder 'what do all these people do?' Increased population will mean more new schools and increasing pressure on existing facilities. To help relieve city centre congestion further a 'southern distributor road' is planned, bypassing Inverness to the east and south. This will involve another river crossing (or possibly a tunnel), in the Holm Mains area, linking to the A82 to Fort William.

It is generally agreed that further transport infrastructure is required in Inverness and there are calls for an integrated bus and rail station. An opportunity to create this was missed in recent years, as the adjacent bus station

Suburban Inverness: Culloden.

at Farraline Park and the railway station backing on to Station Square have both been spruced up, while ignoring each other's proximity completely. In the next decade road links to Inverness Airport will be improved, with dual carriageway most of the way. Perhaps a railway

Looking over Cradlehall to the Moray Firth.

Suburban Inverness: Cradlehall.

station linking directly to the terminal will also become possible. Air links from Inverness can only improve. Locals bemoan the loss of a direct link to London Heathrow, but current thinking makes that unlikely, at least in the foreseeable future. Existing links to Stornoway, Glasgow, Edinburgh, Manchester, Wick, Orkney and Shetland will continue and may expand to include other internal destinations. Charter flights to foreign holiday destinations are welcomed by locals and will likely continue to develop and expand.

Improvements in rail services are planned, though will probably consist of improved facilities and new rolling stock, rather than the massive investment in track which would be required to improve journey times. The Motorail services of the 1970s and 1980s now seem an anachronism, but many Invernessians very much hope that another anachronism – the sleeper service to London – will survive past the first decade of this new century.

In the early years of the 21st century the most spectacular new development has been the expansion of the Eastgate Centre involving the demolition of all the buildings in and around Falcon Square, of which as late as 1970 the authors of the *Third Statistical Account of the country of Inverness* could write:

> 'Falcon Square is the hub of the wholesale trade in Inverness, and here, or in Dempster Gardens, can be found nearly all the goods the people of the north-east and north eat, wear or use in the course of their daily lives.'

Inverness from the Kessock Bridge.

Here were located First, Second, Third and Fourth Street, in an echo of Manhattan, perhaps. Falcon Square takes it name, of course, from the old Falcon Foundry which once stood there. Its principle office block survives, carefully rebuilt off to one side of what is now a public square.

The new Falcon Square is graced with a public monument by local sculptor Gerald Laing, in the form of an obelisk around which falcons swarm – a misrepresentation of the derivation of the name, but an imposing and impressive piece of public sculpture nonetheless. For a while it represented itself as a Mercat Cross (the term used for a market cross in a Scottish burgh) until it was pointed out that Inverness already had a perfectly serviceable mercat cross which stands outside the Town House on High Street. Dating from the middle ages, it is a bit weather-beaten and has suffered in the past from inappropriate attempts at restoration, but at least it has the merit of authenticity.

Inverness has grown over the last 200 years from a small provincial town with tortuous links with the rest of the country to a thriving, though small, city exuding confidence and prosperity. Many people have worked hard over the

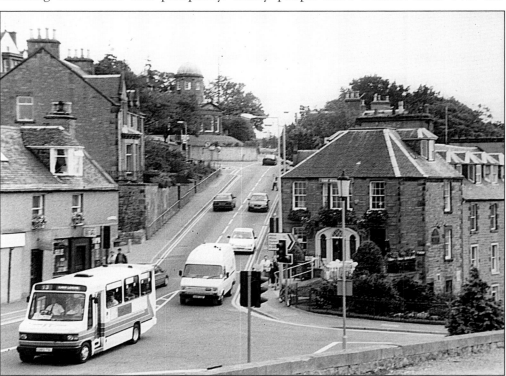

Castle Street: the house at the top of the hill had its own observatory. ©Highland Photographic Archive

years to preserve its past and now we have a chance to ensure that its future has as much architectural merit as today's creative architects can muster. Perhaps there will be an opportunity to repair the cultural vandalism of the 1960s by demolishing the concrete boxes of Bridge Street and replacing them with something more appropriate. Almost certainly a new cultural complex will be built, which will, hopefully, be the realisation of a dream for Invernessians, who are proud of their culture in all its aspects. The new Invernessians will adapt the city to their own, new needs and many remain confident that the next century of change will build on the achievements of the past and will be able to do this without ignoring those achievements and without undervaluing the history and culture which have gone before.

Inverness Castle: prison and courthouse, 1830s, on the site of earlier castles. ©Highland Photographic Archive

FOLKLORE AND
LOCAL TRADITION

LOCAL folklore is a particularly slippery and elusive subject, with a considerable risk of toppling over the boundaries of common sense and credibility into the shady domain of fairy tales and antiquarian wishful thinking. In the local traditions of Inverness there are plenty of examples of both good and bad folklore – fascinating insights into the belief systems of our ancestors coupled with plainly ill-informed nonsense. And then there is Nessie!

Disposing of some of the nonsense first, one of the cherished beliefs of all born and bred Invernessians is that the reason why Inverness was not, until 2001, a city is that the 19th-century Episcopal cathedral was never finished. If only the planned towers or steeples had been added before the money ran out, goes this argument, Inverness could have justly laid claim to city status. There is no truth whatsoever in this assertion. The concept of a city as the seat of a bishop is misplaced. If anything the concept derives from the Roman *civitas* as a centre of civil administration. To be sure, these places often in their subsequent history became centres of ecclesiastical administration too, but the two do not always coincide. In more recent times the growth of industrial centres, especially in England, led to a clamouring for more 'cities'. Now we have regular 'beauty contests' as, sometimes unlikely, candidates compete for a royal warrant, though it might be more realistic to see the award of city status as a political reward.

A very persistent local tradition in Inverness is that the distinctive local accent which is represented as a particularly 'pure' and attractive form of English is due to the Cromwellian garrison which occupied the pentagonal fort overlooking the harbour in the 1640s. This idea was espoused by such eminent visitors as Dr Samuel Johnson and Daniel Defoe. However, a moment's thought would suggest that the kind of English dialect spoken by soldiers in the middle of the 17th century is unlikely to have been particularly attractive, if indeed very comprehensible to the locals at that time. It is also difficult to believe that an occupation by a couple of thousand troops which only lasted for ten years could have such a long-lasting effect. Much more likely, perhaps, is that the local dialect owes much to the fact that for most of its mediaeval and later history Inverness was an island of predominantly English speakers in a sea of Gaelic, developing its distinctive accent and speech patterns in relative isolation, cut off from the Scots and English speakers further south. Also, schooling has always been a high priority in Inverness, with the burgh taking pride in the education of its youngsters. Many of the identifying characteristics of the Invernessian accent are certainly due to the influence of Gaelic, even to the extent of being straight translations of a Gaelic phrase – for example, 'Right enough!' is surely the Gaelic *ceart gu leor.*

As we have seen in the main text, a number of local buildings have wrongly-attributed historical associations. Archaeological investigations at Cromwell's Fort in 2002 revealed that the 'clock tower' preserved on its site was in fact nothing at all to do with the military complex, but was the badly-reconstructed remains of the offices of a later rope factory.

Another persistent local tradition, this time with just the glimmer of a possibility of some historical basis, is that somewhere in Inverness, possibly around about where 'Auldcastle Road' was constructed in the 19th century, is the site of 'Macbeth's Castle'.

Macbeth (Gaelic *mac-Bethad,* 'son of life') was, contrary to Shakespeare's historical caricature, one of the best kings Scotland ever had. Born around 1005, he was a grandson of Malcolm II and married to Gruoch, granddaughter of Kenneth II. He killed Duncan I in 1040 and assumed the throne. His father was the ruler of the province of Moray and his mother was of royal descent. Powerful and prosperous, Macbeth travelled on pilgrimage to Rome in 1050, where he 'scattered alms like seed-corn'.

In the north, before he became king, Macbeth was a *mormaer* – a kind of regional governor who acted on behalf of the monarch. The title survived until supplanted by the arrival of feudalism with the Anglo-Norman invaders in the late 11th century – the first Norman invader of these shores was of course William of Normandy, William the Conqueror, who invaded England in 1066.

In 1054 Siward, Earl of Northumbria, invaded Scotland on behalf of Duncan's son Malcolm, who had found shelter at the court of Edward the Confessor. Siward's English army defeated Macbeth at Dunsinane, in Perthshire. Three years later, fleeing from a second invasion and trying to reach the safety of his strongholds in Moray, Macbeth was cornered at Lumphanan, in Aberdeenshire and killed there. His stepson Lulach, nicknamed 'The Simpleton,' succeeded him but reigned for only a few months before he too was killed and Malcolm took control and ruled as Malcolm III (Malcolm Canmore).

It is very likely that there was a royal castle in Inverness in the 11th century and that, when Macbeth became king, he took control of it. The most likely site is on Castle Hill, which guards the crossing point of the Ness and the entrance to the town. There are some local stories about traces of building stone being found during the construction of Auldcastle Road, but nothing substantial was ever found. Whatever, sadly undocumented, traces there were proved enough to whet antiquarian appetites. If there was a 'castle' in the 11th century, it was most

'King Duncan's Well', near Raigmore Hospital.

probably a timber structure, surrounded by a palisade. The first stone castle in Inverness was probably built in the 12th century, during the reign of David I, if experience in other parts of Scotland is anything to go by.

'King Duncan's Well', on the roadside in Culduthel, adds something to the Macbeth associations, but not very much. Again, archaeological excavations in the area revealed nothing and the well itself is a modern reconstruction. Romantic antiquarianism is the most probable origin of this 'tradition'. Sir Walter Scott has a lot to answer for.

One of the oldest traditions associated with Inverness is, ironically, one of the best documented. When St Columba came north to meet Brude, the king of the Picts, he travelled up the Great Glen to Inverness, probably around 582 AD. There is scant evidence of a Pictish royal stronghold on Craig Phadrig, the Iron Age hill-fort overlooking Inverness, though a little trace of Dark Age squatters there. However, the discovery of an enormous silver chain at the foot of Torvean Hill in 1808, during the construction of the Caledonian Canal, gives that site some credence as the site of King Brude's fort. Unfortunately modern quarrying has removed most of the hilltop.

Torvean is, however, overlooking the Ness, which is where Columba met Nessie, or her ancestor. This episode, one of a series of miraculous encounters described in Adamnan's biography of Columba and designed to enhance his saintly reputation, is interesting in that it took place on the river and not on Loch Ness, where apparently Nessie now resides. Columba's party came across a number of locals mourning the death of a man who, they said, had been attacked by the beast which lived in the river – perhaps more realistically a victim of drowning through cramp in the cold waters? Wishing to cross the river and thereby impress the locals, Columba asked one of his followers to swim across to the other side to collect a small boat. In the middle of the river his disciple was approached by a river monster, with a gaping mouth, moving in for the kill.

Columba raised his arm, made the sign of the cross and commanded the beast to stop, which of course it did and the locals were suitably impressed.

In modern times, Nessie is largely an invention of the media, particularly the *Inverness Courier* which, in 1933, landed its most famous scoop when it reported the sighting of a strange creature in Loch Ness. The newspaper in its issue of 2 May 1933 carried an article with the headline: 'Strange Spectacle on Loch Ness: What was it?' The story was picked up by the national press and the rest, as they say, is history.

Every Invernessian knows about the fairy hill of Tomnahurich, but the origins of the legend are not so well known. In this case we can probably identify the first recorded telling of the fairy tale. In 1891 the Inverness bookseller John Noble published a slender volume of stories and poems under the title *The Witch of Inverness and the Fairies of Tomnahurich*. The author is not identified.

Captain Burt, this anonymous author reminds us, had written about the Hill of Tomnahurich when stationed at Inverness in the 1830s:

'…that prejudiced Londoner, who saw only with the narrow vision of a Cockney, and whose idea of mountain scenery was limited by the gage of Primrose Hill, looked upon our Highland hills and mountains as huge excrescences. In his *'Letters from the North of Scotland,'* written as early as 1735, he mentions Tomnahurich and the traditions attached to it in his time. He thus writes –

"About a mile westward from the town there rises, out of a perfect flat, a very regular hill; whether natural or artificial, I never could find by any tradition; the natives call it *tomman-heurach*. It is almost in the shape of a Thames wherry, turned keel upwards, for which reason they sometimes call it Noah's Ark. The length of it is about four hundred yards, and the breadth at bottom about one hundred and fifty.

From below, at every point of view, it seems to end at the top in a narrow ridge, but when you are there, you find a plain large enough to draw up two or three battalions of men.

Hither we sometimes retire in a summer's evening, and sitting down on the heath, we beat with our hands upon the ground, and raise a most fragrant smell of wild thyme, pennyroyal, and other aromatic herbs, that grow among the heath; and as there is likewise some grass among it, the sheep are fed the first; and when they have eaten it bare, they are succeeded by goats, which browse upon the sweet herbs that are left untouched by the sheep. But this is not the only reason why I speak of this hill; it is the weak credulity with which it is attended, that led me to this detail for as any thing, ever so little extraordinary, may serve as a foundation (to such as are ignorant, heedless, or interested) for ridiculous stories and imaginations. So the fairies within it are innumerable, and witches find it the most convenient place for their frolics and gambols in the night-time.'"

While we are grateful to Captain Burt for recording this example of local folk culture, we could have done without his patronising sneer at the 'credulity' of the ignorant locals. Folklore was an integral part of Gaelic culture, but it was to be another 150 years before scholars were able to place it in its Indo-European context.

At least we know from Burt that there was a local story of fairies associated with Tomnahurich. The little 1891 volume is the first telling of the story which tells of two fiddlers from Strathspey, Farquar Grant and Thomas Cumming, who decided to visit Inverness to raise money to support their families, in a time of want, by busking in the streets. On a cold and frosty December day they headed for the social centre of the town on Bridge Street and began playing, with amazing skill and dexterity. Though they played all day until their fingers were numb with cold, they earned no money. Standing beside the bridge at the foot of Bridge Street, as they bemoaned their wasted day, they were approached by an old man who asked after their families in Tullochgorum. This came as a surprise to the two fiddlers, as the old man was a complete stranger to them, but they replied politely, explaining that they had all fallen on hard times. The old man sympathised with their bad luck and suggested that his folk might enjoy their music. Tired, hungry and now desperate for money, the two fiddlers readily agreed. As they set off across the bridge they struggled to keep up with the sprightly old man as he ascended Tomnahurich Hill. Half way up the hill he stopped at a terrace, beat with his foot on the ground and waved them to enter the doorway of a great illuminated hall. Inside the dazzling hall were tables of glittering glass, in niches of crystal. Each table was piled high with a spectacular feast.

The fiddlers ate and drank until they were full, then were guided onto a platform from where they entertained the hundreds of small, beautiful people in the hall. They played for hours in an atmosphere of festivities and celebration, until at last the old man appeared once more and told them that it was well into the next morning. He guided them to the entrance door and paid them for their exertions giving each of them a purse of gold. Scarcely had they finished thanking the old man when he suddenly disappeared and the two fiddlers found themselves alone on the slopes of Tomnahurich Hill. Both amazed and happy, they returned to Inverness.

The old man's disappearance was not their only surprise. In the rough and uncultivated land they had passed the night before were now fields of waving corn. On approaching the town they found the hovels of the night before replaced by a street of well-built houses, while the old wooden bridge they had crossed was now a stone bridge of seven arches. The citizens of Inverness were dressed in

St Andrew's Cathedral and Tomnahurich Hill. ©Highland Photographic Archive

strange clothes and answered all their questions with jeers and laughter. They were treated as lunatics and impostors.

At length they set off for their native strath – only to find further bewilderment. They recognized nobody and nobody recognized them. Fearing themselves bewitched, they headed for the parish church, where in the graveyard they found the gravestones of the family and friends they had left so recently – all apparently dead for more than a century.

Entering the church, they found a minister they did not know, addressing his congregation. The minister opened his Bible and began a reading, while the congregation stared at the two oddly-dressed interlopers. They continued to watch the fiddlers and, as the minister spoke out loud the name of God, were astonished as the men crumbled into dust before their eyes.

This Inverness Rip Van Winkle story was, we are told in the 1891 book, 'told by a Senachie round the fireside of a Clachnacuddin household 50 years ago to a gathering of wondering youngsters'.

One of them, perhaps our anonymous author, asked if anyone had ever tried to get to the bottom of this strange tale, for example by investigating any strange disappearances. There was indeed a story of an old man whose great-grandfather had lived to a great age and had told of two men from the Strathspey area who had disappeared in Inverness, last seen crossing the old oak bridge in the company of an old man – 'the popular opinion was that the old man who had accosted and decoyed them was the famous Thomas the Rhymer'.

Some say that when the pine trees (or yew trees?) on Tomnahurich were cut down to make way for the development of the present cemetery, the fairies deserted the hill, which explains why they are no longer seen thereabouts.

The spelling and meaning of Tomnahurich has always been problematic. Invernessians call it 'the hill of the fairies', though 'the hill of the yew trees' *(tom na h-iubhraich)* is a more likely derivation from the Gaelic. A possibly apocryphal story tells of an Inverness policeman, in the 1890s, being called upon to record a traffic accident in Tomnahurich Street, where a horse and cart had overturned and seriously injured a passerby. An accident report was required and witnesses were summoned to give their accounts. Enlisting some help, the policeman dragged the remains of the cart a few yards into King Street and began to record events in his notebook, thus avoiding any possibly embarrassing spelling mistakes.

Earliest descriptions of Tomnahurich, the hill of the yew trees, have it covered with pine trees, some of them Scots pine. In the 19th century these were cut down and the hill became the town's cemetery, as the Chapel Yard near the Old High Church was full. Once the flat summit of the hill and the terraced slopes were filled up, the cemetery continued into the flat ground around the base of the hill, where 1500 years ago the Picts had a cemetery. Visitors to Inverness were always directed to the top of Tomnahurich for the outstanding views of Inverness. Originally the view to the north was over the empty fields of Dalneigh. Today the postwar housing runs almost to the base of the hill on the north side. To the south, before the early 1800s, the view was to Torvean and the River Ness winding round its base. Today, Tomnahurich overlooks the Caledonian Canal and the swing road bridge crossing which carries the main road to Fort William winding round the west side of Torvean on its way to Loch Ness.

The cemetery on and around Tomnahurich hill was opened in 1864 as a much needed overflow from the Chapel Yard in Inverness, itself an extension of the original graveyard around the mediaeval parish church. At first burials were on the hilltop and then on the lower slopes, which were terraced. The 'New' Cemetery adjacent to Glenurquhart Road was opened in 1898. The initial development of Tomnahurich cemetery was by the Inverness Cemetery Company, a joint stock company on land feued from the landowner, Baillie of Dochfour. The Burgh of Inverness took over the cemetery in 1909. As available ground reached capacity in the 1990s another extension was started near the new crematorium at Kilvean.

A final example of local folklore, prominent amongst the population until the 1960s and still clinging to life, involves the 'clootie well' at Culloden. Located in the woods above Culloden House and beside the mausoleum of the Forbes of Culloden family, this ancient well is reputed to have magical or healing properties. Supposedly a piece of cloth or clothing (in Scots, a *cloot*) from a person suffering from physical or mental disease should be dipped in the waters of the well and then tied to an adjacent tree. As the cloth rots in the wind and rain, so the disease might be dispelled from the sufferer. To be done properly, it was necessary to be at the well at sunrise on the first day of May, so that the first rays of the morning sun could shine on the cloth. Since at least the 1890s locals have made a mass pilgrimage to the well on the first Sunday in May. Old newspaper accounts speak of thousands of people attending, with special buses laid on from Inverness and Nairn. Many Invernessians remember family outings in the 1950s and 1960s and walking out to Culloden to the well. Coins were thrown into the well for luck and collected at the end of the day for local charities.

In 1878 the Inverness Field Club records a visit to St Mary's Well, or *Tobar na Coille*, the Well of the Wood, on one of its regular excursions. At that time the spring source of the well was encased in a stone basin, which at one time had been covered. A circular stone building surrounded the well, with wooden seats, by now without its conical roof. It was a well with chalybeate (iron salts) in the water, giving a distinctive 'rusty' appearance to the surrounding rocks and it was this property which in all likelihood had attracted the interest of prehistoric people. By 1878 the superstitious May-time practices offended Victorian sensibilities and the popular pilgrimages were denounced from the pulpit and discouraged by the local landowner. On the occasion of the Field Club's visit, however, the trees around the well were festooned with rags and other offerings.

Intriguingly, the Field Club notice of its excursion, published in its Transactions for 12 February 1878, mentions that:

'Many years ago, a pleasant well-kept path conducted the visitor from the high road to this sacred spot, and a woman, possibly yet alive, acted as a kind of priestess, providing dishes, opening the door of the building which guarded the precincts, and generally kept the place and approach in order.'

The Field Club also noted that in 'former times' it was customary for 'a large quota of servant girls and shop lads', amongst others, to set off in crowds from Inverness on the Saturday night, in order to be at the well for sunrise, when the healing magic was at its most efficacious. However the report also concluded that there might have been other, more appealing, motives for visiting the well:

'When we call to mind that there was a public-house, at a distance conveniently near on the line of march, that the throng, consisting of male and female, was a very miscellaneous one indeed, and that no early closing Act was as yet in force, we can more easily imagine than describe the wild scenes of riot and dissipation that were invariably enacted.'

In 1895 Rev Murdo Mackenzie of the Free Presbytery of Inverness drew attention to the 'superstitious practice' of thousands of people making a pilgrimage to the Culloden well. A newcomer to the town, he was 'startled' to find that 3000 persons had visited the shrine the previous Sunday, which he described as 'simply disgraceful'.

At least these pilgrims walked the three miles from Inverness to Culloden under their own steam. By the 1930s the local officers of the Lord's Day Observance Society were drawing attention to the fact that the Traffic

Commissioners had granted licences to three Inverness bus companies allowing them to make special runs to Culloden on the Sabbath. This they regarded as 'an outrage on the feelings of the Christian community'.

That was in 1933. By 1939 they had given up fighting that particular battle but instead wrote to the local paper asking the public:

> 'to refrain from this superstitious practice, and thereby lessen in some measure the already very large volume of Sabbath desecration which is threatening to engulf our beloved land… No doubt some will plausibly affirm that no harm is meant, but that does not alter the fact that we are held accountable, and are meant to attend at another well, even the Well of Salvation spoken of in Scripture.'

Certainly throughout the 1920s and 1930s the annual reports of the pilgrimage to Culloden on the first Sunday in May record thousands of visitors and this continued into the 1960s, after which perhaps the local population became more used to Sunday excursions in their motor cars than long walks in the countryside and the practice declined. In recent years the Barn Church of Culloden (Church of Scotland) has organized a local service at St Mary's Well on the first Sunday in May, but this is hardly the same as a mass pilgrimage.

Perhaps the most poignant pilgrimage was in May 1946, the first year of peace after six years of war. The weather was good and there was a record crowd. Hundreds walked from Inverness, while 'a stream of motor cars from the town and district also arrived at or near the Well'.

There were long queues in Inverness for bus services: Macrae and Dick's buses took 1430 passengers to Culloden from Inverness and over 500 from Nairn, while Alexander's buses conveyed 2846 people. The large crowd was 'well-behaved and good-humoured.'. The sum of £86 and 6 shillings was retrieved from the well and given to the Royal Northern Infirmary and the Highland Orphanage. There was one unusual feature for the local papers to report:

> 'Six Cameron Highlanders, now demobbed, met at the Well in fulfilment of a resolution made at Sfax (in Tunisia) during the North African campaign. When they reached a well in an olive grove at Sfax, they decided that, as it was the first Sunday in May, they would have a ceremony similar to that observed annually at the 'Clootie' Well at Culloden. They drank the water, expressed the wish that they would meet again at the Culloden Well and tied bits of cloth to the olive trees. The wish came true, for Alexander Mackenzie, Robert Mackintosh, Robert Nairn, Alex Patience, Duncan Mackay and John Johnstone were at the Culloden Well on Sunday and drank the water.'
> (*Inverness Courier*, 7 May 1946)

INVERNESS IN EARLY MAPS

A S AN important Royal Burgh in the Highlands it is perhaps not surprising that the town has been well mapped over the years. Maps are the skeleton of local history, the bare bones of a locality, a two-dimensional version of the landscape trapped in time like a fly in amber. Like all historical documents, they have to be assessed for their accuracy and reliability and treated with caution. Maps can be informative, or misleading, or sometimes both at once!

One of the major advances for students of local history in recent years has been the tremendous improvement in access to early maps of a locality. This is due mainly to the professionalism of librarians and archivists, who have always realised the importance of maps to local historians, without always having the resources to make them readily available. Technology has come to the rescue: the invention of the photocopier, good quality photographic reproduction and enlargements and now the appearance of maps in digital format on websites, have all made access possible in ways which quite recently would have seemed science fiction fantasy. Once researchers had to travel to Edinburgh or London to see maps which they can now view on their home computers. This made local history the province of an antiquarian elite who could afford the time and expense involved. Now, the democratisation of local history through the internet, coupled with the commitment of librarians and archivists to take advantage of new technology, has opened up the subject to a wide audience. This brings its own dangers, but the opportunities to bring local expertise to bear are nowhere more evident than in the study of early maps.

In this book we reproduce a selection of early maps covering Inverness, some of them published for the first time. This is not intended to be a complete list of every map covering

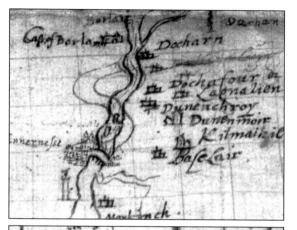

Two versions of Inverness at the end of the 16th century, from manuscript maps by Timothy Pont. ©National Library of Scotland.

Inverness, but the main large-scale maps are all included. We hope that researchers will be encouraged to conduct their own research, using maps available either in paper form or over the internet.

The River Ness appears as a name on Ptolemy's lists, which in the early middle ages were recreated in map form for the emerging Renaissance audience in Europe. However, the first map of Scotland which brought some awareness of the country into the houses of those Europeans who could afford it, was the double folio sheet which appeared in the 1573 edition of Abraham Ortelius's *Theatrum Orbis Terrarum*. Generally regarded as the first 'atlas', this literally put Scotland on the map as a European country.

The Ortelius map is a good example of the dangers of early cartography. The date of the printed map is 1573, but from the density of place-names around the Moray Firth, in Caithness and in Orkney, researchers have deduced that those parts of the map are probably derived from the work of John Elder, a native of Caithness, who in the 1530s produced a map of Scotland for Henry VIII. Ortelius would have used other published maps, printed as single sheets, in his compilation.

There is an expected density of place-names in central Scotland and up the east coast into Aberdeenshire, with a reasonably accurate depiction of the topography, but the Highlands and islands are drawn much more crudely, with few place-names. This suggests that the lowlands and eastern side of Scotland – and Caithness – were the populated and 'civilised' parts of the country, while the highlands and islands were sparsely occupied and uncivilised. This, as we now know, was very far from the truth – the Western Isles and adjacent mainland formed part of the mediaeval territory of the Lords of the Isles, with major cultural achievements in architecture, music, poetry, military organisation and civil administration. The Gaelic-speaking population, though less than their English-speaking compatriots, was substantial and much less sparse than indicated by Ortelius. The result was a map which made a political and social statement which we would now regard as highly questionable.

Ortelius shows Inverness as 'Inuernesse', correctly located at the mouth of the river 'Nessa', but seemingly no more important than the neighbouring settlements of 'Vrchard' (Urquhart), 'Artyrsyre' (Ardersier), 'Chanrye' (Fortrose) and 'Nardyn' (Nairn). It is perhaps worth noting in passing that our spellings of these place-names are equally distant from their Gaelic originals and no less bizarre.

Within 12 years of the Ortelius atlas appearing and perhaps motivated by that and by Saxton's Atlas of England and Wales published in 1579, a young graduate of the University of St Andrews, Timothy Pont, apparently decided to take it upon himself to create an atlas of Scotland. He undertook a series of journeys throughout the entire mainland of Scotland and, it seems, most of the islands, so that from 1585-1595 (the exact dates are unclear) he produced the raw material, the initial surveys and notes, from which the engraved, printed maps would be made. We are lucky in having two versions of the town of Inverness drawn by

Timothy Pont. One appears on sheets depicting the Great Glen, while the other is on a map of the province of Moray.

The Pont manuscript maps of Inverness are important sources of information for the area at the end of the 16th century. All of the place-names in the vicinity of Inverness can still be recognised in today's landscape. The bridge over the river, the castle, the parish church and the early street pattern, can all be traced on these scraps of paper. The ferry to Kessock is shown and on the Longman there is a structure which could reasonably be interpreted as a lighthouse or beacon tower. Unfortunately the detail of the town is somewhat obscured by deletions and amendments on the original, which perhaps made sense to Timothy Pont but for us are difficult to unravel.

Extract from Blaeu's 1654 printed mp 'Extima Scotiae' from the Atlas Novus.

Pont died around 1613 and it was to be 50 years before his manuscript maps were converted into engraved printed maps and published in an atlas. This was eventually achieved in 1654 in Blaeu's (*Atlas Novus*, of which *Volume V* is effectively a county atlas of Scotland. Inverness appears on several sheets, most notably on the sheet covering the whole of northern Scotland and on that of Moray. These printed maps contain far less detail than the Pont manuscripts from which they are derived.

Again, these Blaeu maps raise questions as to dating and as to their use as historical documents. Although they were published in 1654 the information clearly dates from Pont's 1585-95 surveys. We do know that Pont's maps were collated and edited by Robert Gordon, the University of Aberdeen geographer into whose hands the material eventually came. However, because the Blaeu maps are artistic masterpieces in their own right and thus grace many a Highland hotel in Bartholomew reproductions and because this is the depiction of Inverness and the Highlands which was widely disseminated throughout Europe, they are still important in their own right. The Pont maps are more informative, but messier to interpret.

Only a small percentage of Pont's original manuscript maps survive, but those that do, in the care of the National Library of Scotland in Edinburgh, can now be viewed in digital format on their website. They can be enlarged to view detail which previously escaped the notice of researchers. The NLS took the lead in organising Project Pont, which brought a range of disciplines to bear on the Pont problem and produced an impressive amount of research and new results. The most visible result is the digital imagery of the Pont maps, but there were also annual seminars and eventually a book which brought together contributions by a range of experts. The NLS website also includes manuscript sheets in the hand of Robert Gordon, many presumably redrawn from Pont originals, as well as the Blaeu atlas sheets and much else besides.

Extract from Blaeu's 1654 map of Moray and Nairn from the Atlas Novus.

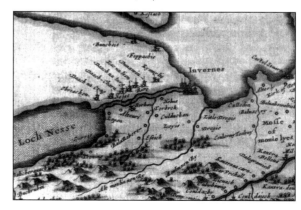

Extract from Moll's county map of Inverness-shire, 1725.

It was to be another hundred years after the publication of Pont's maps in the Blaeu atlas before the Highlands were surveyed again. The Jacobite risings of 1715 and 1745-6 had scared the Government and highlighted the woeful state of cartographic survey of the maze of Highland glens and lochs which afforded Bonnie Prince Charlie such good protection from his pursuers. In the aftermath of Culloden it was clear that there was an urgent requirement on behalf of the British Army to have an accurate and up-to-date survey of Scotland, especially of the Highlands. This task was entrusted to William Roy, an army engineer and surveyor. Between 1747 and 1755 his teams of surveyors covered the whole of the mainland of Scotland (but not the islands), mapping the terrain at the scale of 1 inch to 1,000 yards (1½ inches to 1 mile) in what became known as Roy's Military Survey of Scotland.

The manuscript originals of this survey, which exist in a couple of versions, were top secret military documents in the 18th century. As such, access was limited to military officers and appropriate government officials – and of course the King, in whose Library they were eventually deposited. They are now one of the treasures of the Map Room in the British Library in Paddington.

For years Roy's map was available only to researchers in London. In the 1960s Scottish university libraries were given black and white photocopies of the beautifully coloured original, which were used by generations of cartographic students and historians. More recently, the British Library made the map available on 35mm colour slides, which are spectacular when projected. Colour and black and white copies and photocopies can also be ordered from the British Library.

However, the most dramatic improvement in access to Roy's *Military Survey* came in 2001, when the SCRAN project, which exists to digitise Scotland's

Plan of Inverness in Edward Burt's Letters, *1754.*

cultural heritage, reached a licensing agreement with the British Library and made it available on the SCRAN website. 'Thumbnail' versions of the maps are freely available to anyone, while subscribers can access full size colour images, from which low quality colour copies can be made. Good quality copies are still available only from the British Library.

The Roy map of Inverness

shows a compact, mid-18th-century town, with excellent detail of the street pattern and of the surrounding district. It shows a town that had changed little for hundreds of years, but which in the next hundred years would begin to expand until it was literally bursting at the seams – so that the boundaries of the burgh had to be extended. A prominent feature is the 'Old Fort' at the harbour – the pentangle of Cromwell's Fort, built during the civil wars of the 1640s and already demolished and in ruins by 1747. While in Inverness the surveyors used Balnain House as their base.

For country areas, Roy's Map shows woodlands and most importantly, the extent of arable land. Both of these categories were of military significance. Comparison with estate maps of the same period has shown Roy's *Military Survey* to be generally extremely accurate. Houses are depicted as tiny red rectangles, but it is now generally recognised that although the number of houses in a settlement or township may be accurate, their exact location or disposition may not be. This can be important when trying to

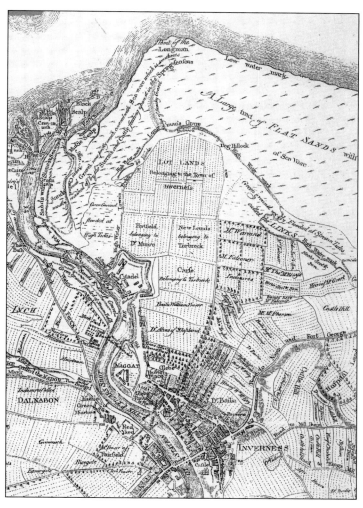

Extract from John Home's map of Inverness, 1774.

match up the ruins of deserted townships with the Roy survey. The Roy map provides a snapshot of the Scottish landscape just before the tremendous reorganisation of the countryside which we call the Agricultural Revolution, with its enclosures and plantings around big 18th-century houses.

It shows Inverness as it was at the time of the Battle of Culloden, which took place on 16 April 1746 a mile up the hill from Culloden House, on Drumossie Moor. Both of these features are depicted, but there is no mention of the battle.

The first town plan of Inverness appears in a printed book, Edward Burt's *Letters from a Gentleman in the North of Scotland to his Friend in London* (1754). It shows only the centre of the town, with the castle and the bridge prominent.

The first complete town plan, published on a separate sheet, was John Home's survey of 1774. This is the first map to show the detail of the townscape of Inverness and of the surrounding landscape which of course is now entirely built on. Of particular interest is the detail of the river, with its fishing pools. Just two years later, in 1776, the Taylor and Skinner route maps of the roads of Scotland were published. Inverness occurs several times and although it was not the purpose of these road maps to give a detailed town plan, there are some interesting details – for example the town gallows, located at the top of Castle Street.

Extracts from Taylor & Skinner's route maps, 1776; the one in the centre shows the town gibbet, at the top of Castle Street.

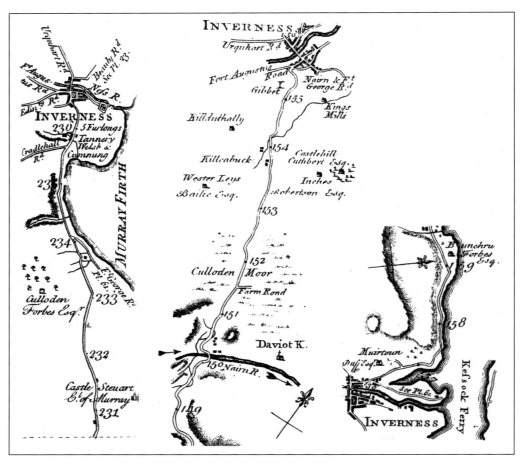

One of Scotland's most prolific town surveyors was John Wood, whose 1821 plan of Inverness does not cover such a large area as Home's plan of 1774, but which is of great interest in showing developments over that period of 47 years. This is Inverness poised on the brink of expansion. With the passage of the Reform Bill of 1832 which extended the franchise to some residents of burghs, it was necessary for the legislators to define the extent of burghs and to map their exact boundaries, also described in words. Allowing what they thought was a generous amount of land for expansion, a map of Inverness was published in 1832 in the report of the government body charged with implementing the new Act of Parliament. This map shows that nobody at that time, in their wildest imaginings, could have predicted the later growth of Inverness, especially at the end of the 20th century.

The last useful mapping of Inverness and its environs was published in John Thomson's *1832 Atlas of Scotland*, though the Inverness-shire sheets were in fact printed and sold separately in 1830.

Extract from John Wood's town plan of Inverness, 1821.

From the time of the anticipated invasion of the south coast of Britain by the French during the Napoleonic Wars the government responsibility for a new, large-scale survey of the country had rested with the Board of Ordnance. The name explains the military interest in maps – if you are trying to lob an artillery shell on top of an enemy position it is essential to know the exact distance from the target. In the middle of the 19th century the decision was taken by what was then known as the Ordnance Survey to map the entire country at the scale of 6 inches to 1 mile, or 1:10,560. The first edition of this OS map of Inverness dates from the 1870s, with a second edition in the early 1900s. Both editions can be viewed in full at Inverness Library, where they are stored under the care of Highland Archives.

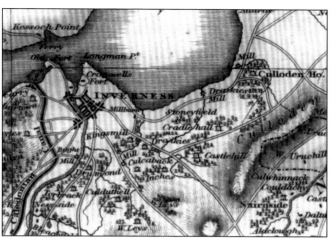

Extract from John Thompson's 1830 map of Inverness-shire, published in his Atlas of Scotland, 1832.

It was also decided to produce maps at the larger scale of 25 inches to one mile, using the same survey, for areas of settlement only. This, of course, includes Inverness and the surrounding districts. And for the burgh itself, a plan at the scale of 50 inches to one mile was produced – it shows every pillar box and manhole cover. These large scale maps also show the internal arrangements of buildings – except where there were security issues, as with prisons!

At the end of the 19th century, with the growth of mass tourism, the Ordnance Survey realised there was a market for smaller scale maps, so the familiar 1 inch to 1 mile series was produced, soon to be followed by the 2½ inches to 1 mile maps beloved of generations of hill-walkers. In the 1930s the National Grid was added, allowing places to be located very exactly indeed with 6-figure or 8-figure map references – grid references, still part of the vocabulary of modern cartography. Then, in the 1970s, the decision was taken to 'go metric' and the 1:50,000 sheets replaced the old 1 inch to 1 mile series – something which did not meet with universal approval. This scale was remarkably similar to William Roy's choice in the middle of the 18th century. The walkers'

Part of Inverness from the First edition of the OS 6"=1 mile map, 1874.

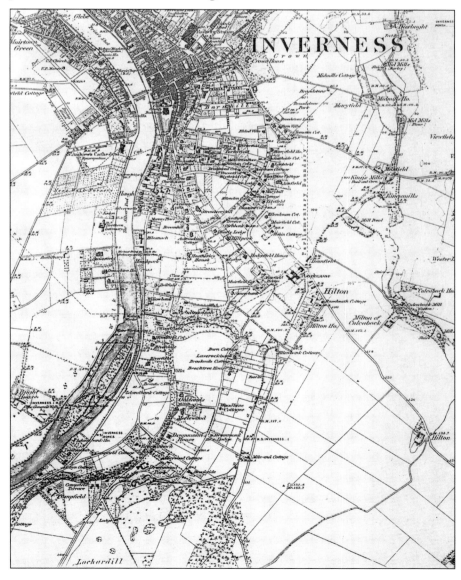

maps survived at the metric scale of 1:25,000, while the old 6 inches to 1 mile (1:10,560) maps reappeared, completely resurveyed, at 1:10,000. Today, large scale maps are difficult – and expensive – to obtain in paper format, but are readily available in digital format, customised to the user's needs and specifications.

Part of Inverness from the Second edition of the OS 6"=1 mile map, 1902.

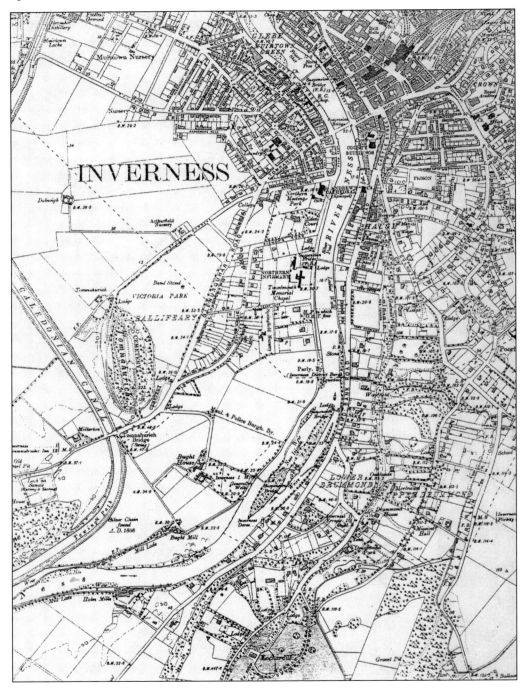

INVERNESS PLACE NAMES

Inverness	*Inbhirnis*	the mouth of the Ness
Balloch	*Baile an loch*	farm of the loch
Allanfearn	*An t-ailean fearna*	green of the alder
Petty	*Peit*	homestead
Tornagrain	*Torr nan gran*	hill of the grain
Dalcross	*Dealg an rois*	prickly point or wood
Ardersier	*Aird nan saor*	headland of the carpenter
Balnagowan	*Baile nan gobhainn*	farm of the smiths
Resaurie	*An ruigh samhraidh*	summer grazing
Culloden	*Cuil lodair*	nook of the marsh
Clava	*Clach mhath*	good stone
Croy	*Cruaidh*	hard place
Kildrummie	*Coille droma*	wood of the ridge
Culcabock	*Cuil na cabaig*	nook of the cheese
Inshes	*meadows*	
Balvonie	*Baile a'mhonaidh*	moorland farm
Muckovie	*Mucomhaigh*	pig field
Bogbain	*Bog ban*	white bog
Daviot	*Deimidh*	a strong place
Achnahillin	*Ach na h-iodhlainn*	field of the stackyard
Meallmore	*Meall mor*	large round hill
Auchnagall	*Ach nan Gall*	field of the strangers
Moy	*Moighe*	plain
Tomatin	*Tom aitinn*	juniper hillock
Balnespick	*Baile an easbuig*	Bishop's farm
Tordarroch	*Torr darach*	hill of the oak
Balloan	*Baile loin*	farm of the wet meadows
Dunlichity	*Dun fhluich aite*	fort of the wet place
Flichity	*Fluich aite*	wet place
Duntelchaig	*Dun an t-sealachaig*	fort of the snail
Inverernie	*Inbhir fhearna*	mouth of the alder burn
Croachy	*Cruach aite*	place of peaks
Ruthven	*Ruadh bheinn*	red mountain
Gorthleck	*Gort a'ghlaic*	field of the hollow
Boleskine	*Both fhleisginn*	farm of the willows
Foyers	*Foithear*	slope
Clachnaharry	*Clach na h-aire*	stone of the watching
Bogroy	*Bog ruadh*	red bog
Phoineas	*Bho an eas*	under the waterfall
Lovat	*Loth ait'*	rotten place
Ballifeary	*Baile na faire*	the farm of the watching
Balnafettach	*Baile nam feadag*	farm of the plovers
Castle Heathe	*Caisteal lethoir*	castle of the slope
Clachnacuddin	*Clach na Cudainn*	stone of the tubs
Culduthel	*Cuil daothail*	nook of Duthil
Dalneigh	*Dal an eich*	horse field
Leachkin	*An Leacainn*	the hillside
Raigmore	*Rathaig mhor*	the large fortified farm
Scorguie	*Sgorr gaoithe*	windy point
Tomnahurich	*Tom na h-iubraich*	hill of the yew trees
Torvean	*Torr Bheathain*	hill of St Bean

INDEX